The place of greatest glory

JOHN 13–21

by Josh Moody

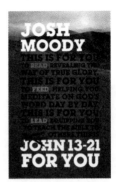

John 13-21 For You

If you are reading *John 13–21 For You* alongside this Good Book Guide, here is how the studies in this booklet link to the chapters of *John 13–21 For You*:

Study One → Ch 1   Study Five → Ch 6
Study Two → Ch 2   Study Six → Ch 7-8
Study Three → Ch 3-4   Study Seven → Ch 9
Study Four → Ch 5   Study Eight → Ch 10

Find out more about *John 13–21 For You* at:
www.thegoodbook.com/for-you

The place of greatest glory
The Good Book Guide to John 13–21
© Josh Moody/The Good Book Company, 2019.
Series Consultants: Tim Chester, Tim Thornborough,
                    Anne Woodcock, Carl Laferton

Published by:
The Good Book Company

thegoodbook.com | thegoodbook.co.uk
thegoodbook.com.au | thegoodbook.co.nz | thegoodbook.co.in

Unless indicated, all Scripture references are taken from the Holy Bible, New International Version. Copyright © 2011 Biblica. Used by permission.

A CIP catalogue record for this book is available from the British Library.

ISBN: 9781784983611 | Printed in Turkey

Design by André Parker

CONTENTS

Introduction: Good Book Guides

Every Bible-study group is different—yours may take place in a church building, in a home or in a cafe, on a train, over a leisurely mid-morning coffee or squashed into a 30-minute lunch break. Your group may include new Christians, mature Christians, non-Christians, moms and tots, students, businessmen or teens. That's why we've designed these *Good Book Guides* to be flexible for use in many different situations.

Our aim in each session is to uncover the meaning of a passage, and see how it fits into the "big picture" of the Bible. But that can never be the end. We also need to appropriately apply what we have discovered to our lives. Let's take a look at what is included:

⊕ **Talkabout:** Most groups need to "break the ice" at the beginning of a session, and here's the question that will do that. It's designed to get people talking around a subject that will be covered in the course of the Bible study.

⊥ **Investigate:** The Bible text for each session is broken up into manageable chunks, with questions that aim to help you understand what the passage is about. The **Leader's Guide** contains **guidance for questions**, and sometimes ⊻ additional "follow-up" questions.

⊡ **Explore more (optional):** These questions will help you connect what you have learned to other parts of the Bible, so you can begin to fit it all together like a jig-saw; or occasionally look at a part of the passage that's not dealt with in detail in the main study.

→ **Apply:** As you go through a Bible study, you'll keep coming across **apply** sections. These are questions to get the group discussing what the Bible teaching means in practice for you and your church. ⊡ **Getting personal** is an opportunity for you to think, plan and pray about the changes that you personally may need to make as a result of what you have learned.

↑ **Pray:** We want to encourage prayer that is rooted in God's word—in line with his concerns, purposes and promises. So each session ends with an opportunity to review the truths and challenges highlighted by the Bible study, and turn them into prayers of request and thanksgiving.

The **Leader's Guide** and introduction provide historical background information, explanations of the Bible texts for each session, ideas for **optional extra** activities, and guidance on how best to help people uncover the truths of God's word.

Why study John 13–21?

"These [things] are written that you may believe that Jesus is the Messiah, the Son of God, and that by believing you may have life in his name."
                                                              (John 20:31)

Welcome to the second part of John's Gospel—what is known as the "book of glory". In chapters 1 – 12, the "book of signs," John described the miracles that Jesus did that pointed to himself as the Son of God. Now, from chapter 13 onward, the hour has come for Jesus to be glorified (12:23). Yet the place of greatest glory is deeply counter-intuitive: the Messiah's glory will come through the cross. And it is by believing in him that we have life—life to the full (10:10).

As chapter 13 opens, we are in Jerusalem with Jesus. It is the Passover. Right at the start of the Gospel, John the Baptist declared that Jesus is the Lamb of God, who takes away the sin of the world (1:29), and that promise is now going to be fully fulfilled. We will follow along as Jesus prepares his disciples for what is about to happen: washing their feet, promising them the Holy Spirit, calling them to remain in him, and praying for them, and for us. This is some of the richest teaching that we will hear from the mouth of our Lord.

Then we come to the pinnacle of John's Gospel: Jesus' crucifixion. Yet through the twists and turns of the narrative, we see that it is not a tragedy but a victory. But it is a victory that comes about through a most unlikely event: the sacrificial death of the hero of the story. And it is a victory that is ultimately displayed by Jesus' wonderful, death-defeating, peace-bringing resurrection three days later.

John 13 – 21 calls us to follow Jesus in order to have the life to the full that he offers. That following will involve sacrifice—dying to ourselves—as Jesus tells Peter in the Gospel's powerful closing chapter. But we'll see that life in Jesus' name is the only life worth having; indeed, it is the only real life at all.

So read on and enter into the book of glory: a glory which the world has never known, but which those who believe in the Son of God will have an eternity to look on, face to face.

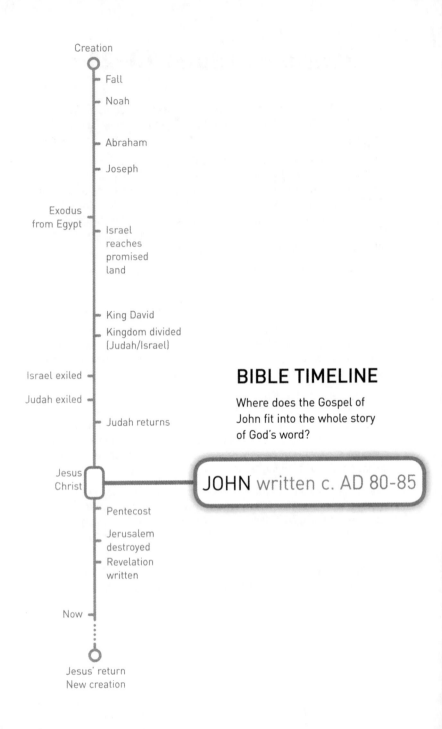

Creation

Fall

Noah

Abraham

Joseph

Exodus from Egypt

Israel reaches promised land

King David

Kingdom divided (Judah/Israel)

Israel exiled

Judah exiled

Judah returns

BIBLE TIMELINE

Where does the Gospel of John fit into the whole story of God's word?

Jesus Christ

JOHN written c. AD 80-85

Pentecost

Jerusalem destroyed

Revelation written

Now

Jesus' return
New creation

1

John 13:1-38
POWER TO SERVE

⊕ talkabout

1. Have you ever seen someone in a position of power do something unexpected? What was it, and what made it so surprising?

⊕ investigate

▶ Read John 13:1-17

This whole section of John begins with a time marker: "It was just before the Passover Festival" (v 1). John's first readers knew that Jesus had died at Passover, so John uses this phrase to turn our minds toward that event as we read this episode.

2. What is it that is moving Jesus both to go to the cross and to wash his disciples' feet (v 1)? Why is this extraordinary?

3. Look at the way John describes this moment in verses 3-5. What is so shocking about what Jesus does?

4. Why does Peter object to having his feet washed, do you think (v 6-8)? What has he misunderstood about Jesus?

• What is it that makes him change his mind (v 8-9)? What has he rightly understood about Jesus?

5. In what way is this footwashing…

• a picture of the love Christ will show on the cross (v 10-11)?

• an example of the love he expects his people to demonstrate (v 12-15)?

Verse 10 is a little complicated but readily explicable. The Christian does not need a "bath" anymore—they have been born again by God's Spirit and are in Christ. But they do still need on occasion to receive forgiveness through regular repentance and confession of their sins (as in 1 John 1:8-9).

⮕ apply

Jesus is showing his disciples how God's authority and power should be revealed in loving, humbling service: "I have set you an example that you should do as I have done for you" (13:15).

6. Think about some of the things you do for others at church, home or work. How can we tell whether our actions are genuine acts of service?

7. What two motivations does Jesus give for us to serve others in this way (v 16-17)?

• How will these help you to be increasingly servant-hearted?

⬇ **investigate**

▶ **Read John 13:18-30**

8. Why does Jesus tell his disciples that he is going to be betrayed (v 19)?

9. How does this incident show God's total sovereign control over the events that are about to unfold?

• Verse 18

• Verse 21

• Verse 26

• Verse 27

⊡ **explore more**

optional

Why did Judas do it? There are many possible explanations for Judas' betrayal of his Lord. At a human level, we know it was at least partly done out of greed (John 12:6). But there was another level of motivation too—a spiritual dynamic; the devil was at work (13:2, 27).

▶ **Read 1 Peter 5:8-11**

What does Peter warn Christians about?
Do you, and Christians you know, give much thought to this prowling lion? Why is that, do you think?
What does Peter tell us to do?

One of the great tragedies in John 13 is that, at least in principle, Judas could have repented. But now the die is cast and it is too late. There can come a moment when you so harden your heart to the truth of God that the course of your life is set. Be warned—when you say no to Jesus and yes to evil, there may come a time when you can no longer say yes to Jesus.

> **Read John 13:31-38**

10. Where and how will God's glory be most clearly displayed (v 31-32)?

DICTIONARY

Son of Man (v 31): Jesus often used this title to refer to himself (see Daniel 7 v 13-14).
Glorified (v 31): Christ's greatness would be revealed at the cross.

• How is this different to the way we normally think about glory?

11. Jesus has clear foreknowledge of both Judas' betrayal and Peter's denial. How does this make his earlier foot-washing even more remarkable?

⮊ **apply**

"A new command I give you: love one another. As I have loved you, so you must love one another. By this everyone will know that you are my disciples, if you love one another." (v 34-35)

12. To what extent is your church characterized by this kind of love?

- Instead of love, what other things are you in danger of prizing more dearly as a church?

- What would it look like for you to move closer to the vision that Jesus has for his church?

⊞ pray

- Praise Jesus for his power—he is the one who has "all things under his power" (v 3).

- Thank Jesus for his love—that he was willing to lay down that power in order to love his people "to the end" and to make them clean (v 1).

- Pray that, as a church, you would also be those who use your power to serve and to love one another.

2 John 14:1-31
PROMISES FOR TROUBLED HEARTS

The story so far

Jesus washed his disciples' feet and told them to serve and love one another. He warned that Judas would betray him and Peter would deny him.

⊕ talkabout

1. Can you think of a time when a respected leader announced they were leaving? How did it feel? What kinds of things helped to smooth the transition in leadership?

⊙ investigate

> **Read John 14:1-4**

DICTIONARY

My Father's house (v 2): heaven, where God dwells.

2. How does Jesus expect his disciples to be feeling at this moment (v 1)? Why might they be feeling this way?

3. What promise does Jesus make to comfort them?

• What is he talking about? Why does he choose this image, do you think?

• What will it take for Jesus to "prepare a place" in heaven for the disciples?

⊡ getting personal

Heaven is not a generic praise and worship service. So valuable does Jesus consider you that he prepares a place *specifically for you* in heaven.

In what area of your life do you need to let this promise give you comfort?

In verse 4 Jesus somewhat cryptically suggests that the disciples know the way to the place where he is going. Then Thomas gives voice to the question that is probably on everyone's mind…

❯ Read John 14:5-14

4. Jesus makes a big claim in response to Thomas's question. What is it (v 6)?

• What are some of the implications of this claim?

5. How would you sum up what Jesus says in verses 7-11 in one sentence?

• What is the link between this and what Jesus has just said in verses 1-6?

What does it mean to do "even greater things" than Jesus' miracles (v 12)? He cannot mean greater quantity or quality of miracles, but a greater kind of miracle. The key is the phrase "because I am going to the Father" (v 12). This will lead to the sending of the Spirit (see John 16:7). So the "greater things" refers to the evangelization of the world, leading to the greatest possible miracle—the work of the Spirit in bringing saving faith. Jesus died alone, with only a few disciples following him. Now the Christian church spans the globe and numbers in the millions.

⮕ apply

6. What is it about verse 6 that is so controversial in our culture today? Have you come across this attitude in your own experience?

• What is the good news in verse 6? How can we make sure we communicate that positively?

7. What truths do you see in these verses that motivate you toward more urgent evangelism?

⬇ investigate

❯ Read John 14:15-31

8. What do the following verses tell us about the Holy Spirit?

    • v 16

    • v 17a

    • v 17b

    • v 18

    • v 26

9. What link does Jesus draw between love and obedience (v 15, 21, 23-24)?

• Is that normally how we think? Why / why not?

• How does Jesus model perfect loving obedience to his Father (v 30-31)?

10. In verse 27 Jesus says for a second time, "Do not let your hearts be troubled" (see also v 1). How would you summarize…

• the reasons he has given his disciples to not be troubled?

• the authority with which he makes those statements?

⊡ **explore more**

optional

This passage, along with others in John, raises lots of questions about the nature of the Trinity and how the Father and the Son relate to one another.

▶ **Read John 1:1-2, 5:19-20, 6:38, 10:30, 14:11; 14:28; 14:31**

What do these verses reveal about the relationship of the Father and the Son?
How does this move you to worship the triune God more deeply?

⤷ apply

11. Since the apostles were inspired by the Spirit to write the New Testament, what implications does that have for how we approach the Bible?

- When have you experienced the Spirit giving you comfort in troubled times through the pages of Scripture?

⬆ pray

"And I will do whatever you ask in my name, so that the Father may be glorified in the Son. You may ask me for anything in my name, and I will do it." (John 14:13-14)

To ask for something in Jesus' name means to ask for the things that Jesus wants to happen and that reflect Jesus' desires and purposes.

Think about some of the things Jesus promises in this passage, and then confidently ask your Father in heaven to do them, in Jesus' name.

3 John 15:1 – 16:33
FRUIT THAT WILL LAST

The story so far

Jesus washed his disciples' feet and told them to serve and love one another. He warned that Judas would betray him and Peter would deny him.

Jesus told the disciples that he was going away to prepare a place for them in his Father's house; but in his absence, he would send the Holy Spirit.

⊕ talkabout

1. What is the key to being fruitful at work?

• What about in the Christian life?

⊕ investigate

❱ Read John 15:1-17

2. What is meant by each of the elements in this metaphor?

• The vine (v 1)

DICTIONARY

Vine (v 1): a climbing plant that grows grapes.
Prunes (v 2): trims back, so as to encourage growth.

- The gardener (v 1)

- The branches (v 5)

- The fruit (v 5-8; look at what Jesus goes on to talk about in particular in verses 9-17)

3. What does Jesus say is key to being fruitful as a Christian?

- v 2

- v 4-5

- v 7-8

- v 9-11

• v 16

⤷ **apply**

4. How is what Jesus says in these verses…

• a relief?

• a warning?

• something to be excited about?

⊡ **getting personal**

Our relationship with Christ, our connection to the vine, our remaining in him through faith and trust, time in God's word and in prayer—all that is the key to fruitfulness.

Are you "remaining" in Christ through his word, through obedience to his commands, through love, through prayer? How could you prioritize remaining in Christ more?

⊌ investigate

Belonging to Jesus, the true vine, should cause his followers to love one another. But now Jesus warns his disciples that they will face hatred too…

❯ Read John 15:18 – 16:15

5. What kind of reaction can the disciples expect from "the world" (15:18; 16:2)? Why (15:19-25)?

⊡ explore more

optional

❯ Read Psalm 35:17-21; Psalm 69:1-4

These are both psalms written by David. Why does Jesus choose to identify himself with this Old Testament king by quoting these psalms in John 15:25, do you think?

6. What are the disciples called to do in the face of this opposition (15:26 – 16:15)?

7. What else does Jesus promise in order to help them (15:26-27; 16:7-15)?

8. Why is Jesus telling his disciples these things (16:1)?

📖 **explore more**

optional

> **Re-read John 16:7-11**

What is the Spirit's role in the world (v 8)?
In order to be saved, what is it that we must understand about...
• sin (v 9)?
• righteousness (v 10)?
• judgment (v 11)?
How should these verses...
• shape what we pray about for our non-Christian friends?
• shape what we say to our non-Christian friends?

> **Read John 16:16-33**

9. What does Jesus say is going to happen soon (v 16)? What does he mean by this?

DICTIONARY

Speaking figuratively (v 25): using imagery and metaphors that are not to be taken literally.

10. What does Jesus say about joy in verses 19-24? Why do you think he chooses to say this to his disciples now?

11. Look at verses 25-33. How does what Jesus says here re-emphasize some of the things we've already seen in John 13 – 16?

→ **apply**

12. Have you experienced hatred for being a disciple of Jesus? If so, what did it look like?

- What truths from this passage will we need to remind ourselves of next time we face opposition from the world?

↑ **pray**

Pray that you would be those who joyfully remain in Christ and love one another, even in the face of opposition.

Pray for non-Christians you know, asking the Spirit to convict them about sin, righteousness and judgment.

Pray for Christians facing hatred or persecution from "the world" in a particular area of the globe.

4 John 17:1-26
A TIME FOR GLORY

The story so far

Jesus washed his disciples' feet and told them to serve and love one another. He warned that Judas would betray him and Peter would deny him.

Jesus told the disciples that he was going away to prepare a place for them in his Father's house; but in his absence, he would send the Holy Spirit.

Jesus told the disciples to remain in him and love one another—even though the world would hate them because they belonged to him.

⊕ talkabout

1. Describe your prayer life in three words.

For most of us, prayer is something that it is easier to talk about than to do. But not so with Jesus. He practices what he preaches. In his prayer in John 17 we find a model of prayer to encourage and equip us.

⊕ investigate

▶ Read John 17:1-5

2. What does Jesus mean when he says that "the hour has come" (v 1)?

3. Who is the focus of this first section of prayer? Why do you think that is?

• What specifically does Jesus pray for (v 5)?

4. What do these verses reveal about the workings of the Trinity?

▶ **Read John 17:6-19**

5. Who is the focus of this second section of prayer?

• Why do you think that is? (What is Jesus aiming for in v 8, 11a, 13?)

• What specifically does Jesus pray for (v 11, 15, 17)?

⊡ explore more

John 17 would not be the last time Jesus prayed for his disciples.

▶ **Read Romans 8:33-34**

What is Jesus doing right now?
Where is he, and why is that significant?
About what, in particular, should this give us confidence, according to these verses? Why?

⊡ getting personal

"Sanctify them by the truth; your word is truth" (v 17).

What sin are you struggling with? Ask yourself this question: what lie am I believing? Behind sinful habits there is always a lie, and the tool for release is always "by the truth; your word is truth."

⊖ apply

6. Look at verses 15-16. How do you think you're doing with being *in* the world but not *of* the world? In what ways do you struggle to get the balance right?

⊙ investigate

▶ **Read John 17:20-26**

7. Who is the focus of this third section of prayer (v 20)?

8. What specifically does Jesus pray for, and why?

• v 21-23

• v 24

• v 26

explore more

Church unity is important to Jesus.

❯ **Read Ephesians 4:1-6**

*Why do you think we are told to "keep" unity, not create unity (v 3)?
What does that imply?
What would it look like for you to "make every effort" to maintain unity
within your church family? (Look at v 2 and 4-6 for ideas.)*

getting personal

Jesus' prayer, and his purpose, is that we would see his glory and be
with him in glory for all eternity (v 24). Reflecting on our future gives us
the strength to keep on going with joy in the here and now. How might
you reflect more on the truths of verse 24 day by day?

9. From what we've seen in John 17, describe Jesus' prayer life in three words.

⤷ apply

10. How could you make your prayer life more closely resemble Jesus' model here? In particular, think about...

• who you pray for.

• what you pray for.

⬆ pray

Thank God for Jesus, who went to the cross to give us eternal life. Then pray...

• for one another, that you would be protected from the evil one and be growing in sanctification.
• for your church, thanking God for the unity you share and asking God to help you maintain it.
• for other churches in your local area, asking God to help you to be united in the gospel as you seek to make Christ known.
• for non-Christians you know, that they would come to "believe in [Jesus] through [your] message" (v 20).

5 John 18:1-27
BETRAYAL AND DENIAL

The story so far

Jesus told the disciples that he was going away to prepare a place for them in his Father's house; but in his absence, he would send the Holy Spirit.

Jesus told the disciples to remain in him and love one another—even though the world would hate them because they belonged to him.

Jesus prayed for his disciples, and for all who would become Christians after them—for their sanctification, unity, and love, for the glory of God.

⊕ talkabout

1. In what kinds of situations or relationships are you most tempted to speak or act as if you don't know Jesus?

Denying Jesus is not something that any Christian wants to do. But what happens when, despite our best intentions, we do something that, in effect, does deny Jesus? John 18 tells a famous story of failure—but there is hope of forgiveness too.

⊕ investigate

❯ Read John 18:1-14

2. Where does this scene take place? How does Judas know he will find Jesus there?

> **DICTIONARY**
>
> **Detachment (v 3):** group.
> **The cup (v 11):** represents God's wrath—his just anger at sin.

• Why does this make his betrayal even more shocking?

3. Look at verse 4. If Jesus knows what is about to happen, why does he ask the crowd who they want?

4. Twice the mob say they have come for "Jesus of Nazareth." What do Jesus' two responses tell us about him?

• v 5-6

• v 8-9

5. Why does Jesus tell Peter to put his sword away (v 10-11)?

6. What details in verses 13-14 suggest that Jesus' trial will not be a fair one?

⊡ explore more

Verse 14 is a reference to a conversation in the Sanhedrin, recorded earlier in John.

> **▶ Read John 11:47-53, 3:16, 1:29**

In what sense was Caiaphas right?
Why do you think John chooses to remind us of this detail in 18:14?
How does it help us to understand what is going on?
What does it teach us about the way God works?

⊡ getting personal

Jesus is the one whose voice can make armed men fall over, yet he allowed himself to be bound and led away so that not one of his people would be lost. How does that make you feel?

⊖ apply

7. Jesus is powerful in the face of opposition, and yet submits to his Father's will. He knows that his Father is sovereign over what he is about to suffer and will use evil to achieve good purposes. How should that mindset help you to have peace in the face of trouble?

⊍ investigate

> **▶ Read John 18:15-27**

8. What is striking about how events unfold in the courtyard (v 15-18, 25-27)?

DICTIONARY
Another disciple (v 15): an unnamed follower of Jesus; possibly John.

• How well does Peter stand up under questioning?

9. How well does Jesus stand up under questioning in verses 19-24?

• Put his replies in your own words.

10. Why does John put verses 19-24 between the two scenes in the courtyard, do you think?

⊡ **getting personal**

Can you think of a time when, out of fear, you denied Jesus or acted as though you didn't know him?

⊡ apply

11. "Peter was just as bad as Judas." Do you agree? Why / why not?

- Satan would love to convince us that our denials make us a Judas, not a Peter. How does the ending of Peter's story (see John 21:15-19) help us when we feel guilty for letting Jesus down?

At the very same time as Peter denied knowing Christ, Christ stood firm on the truth, walking deliberately to the death that would win forgiveness for that very denial. It was cold that night (18:18); but Christ's love for his people burned still.

12. How does Christ's faithfulness help us to stay faithful under pressure?

⬆ pray

Thank Christ for faithfully facing death on your behalf.

Pray for any situations or relationships in which you are tempted to deny Christ or act as though you don't know him—pray for his help to stay faithful, and to enjoy his full forgiveness when you fail.

Pray for persecuted Christians around the world who face violence and unjust prosecution as they follow in the steps of their suffering Savior. Pray that they would not deny Christ, but stay faithful

6

THE GLORY OF THE CROSS

The story so far

Jesus told the disciples to remain in him and love one another—even though the world would hate them because they belonged to him.

Jesus prayed for his disciples, and for all who would become Christians after them—for their sanctification, unity, and love, for the glory of God.

With the help of Judas, the religious leaders arrested Jesus. Jesus went willingly and spoke truthfully under trial, but Peter denied even knowing him.

⊕ talkabout

1. "Looks can be deceiving." How have you seen this play out when it comes to the areas of weakness and strength?

Jesus has just undergone an overnight trial involving the Jewish high priest and his cronies. As the sun rises, Jesus is brought before Pilate, the Gentile governor.

⊕ investigate

> **Read John 18:28 – 19:16**

2. When are these events happening (18:28)? Why is that significant?

DICTIONARY

Ceremonial uncleanness (v 28): a state that would prevent a Jew from taking part in religious ceremonies.

Charges (v 29): accusations.

Caesar (19 v 12): the Roman Emperor.

Day of Preparation (v 14): Friday, the day before the Sabbath.

3. These verses describe a tense courtroom drama, with Jesus' life hanging in the balance. But who is really in control of the action?

For each party, note in the left-hand column the verse references or details that suggest they are in a position of power. Then note in the right-hand column the verse references or details that suggest they are in a position of weakness.

	POWER	WEAKNESS
JEWISH LEADERS		
PILATE		
JESUS		

4. So, who killed Jesus?

⊡ **explore more**

optional

> **Read Isaiah 53:1-9**

What elements of Isaiah's prophecy do you see being fulfilled in John 18:28 – 19:16?
What does Isaiah's prophecy tell us about why all this happened?

➔ **apply**

"Crucify! Crucify!" These are words spoken by creatures of their Creator.

5. What does this passage show you about your sin, and about your own need for a Saviour?

⊡ **getting personal**

Barabbas, whose name means "son of the father," goes free, while Jesus, the Son of the Father, is sentenced to death. The rebel is set free because the innocent substitute dies in his place. So it is with us.

What do you want to say to Jesus in response?

⊡ **investigate**

> **Read John 19:16-30**

DICTIONARY

Hyssop (v 29): a type of wild shrub.

6. What do the following verses show us about Jesus, and the purpose of his death?

• v 19-22

• v 23-24

• v 25-27

• v 28-30

⊡ **explore more**

> **Read Psalm 22**

In what way does this psalm point forward to the crucifixion account in John's Gospel?
Why does it matter that the death of Jesus was no accident but a planned and prophesied event?

> **Read John 19:31-42**

DICTIONARY

Have the legs broken (v 31): a way of speeding up the criminal's death.

7. How does John show us that Jesus was really dead (v 31-37, 38-42)?

• Why is that important, do you think?

8. What is the significance of the Scripture that John quotes in verses 36-37?

⤷ apply

"It is finished." Our salvation is secure. The price has been paid—in full, complete, done, *finished*.

9. In what ways do we sometimes think or act as though it is *not* finished?

• What will it look like to live out the words "It is finished" this week?

10. Jesus said that whoever wants to be his disciple must "take up their cross and follow" him (Mark 8:34). How has reading this passage about your crucified King challenged your expectations of what following him will look like?

⬆ **pray**

Spend time worshiping Jesus, the King who died in your place, before praying through the things you discussed in response to questions 9 and 10.

7 John 20:1-31
LIFE IN HIS NAME

The story so far

Jesus prayed for his disciples, and for all who would become Christians after them—for their sanctification, unity, and love, for the glory of God.

With the help of Judas, the religious leaders arrested Jesus. Jesus went willingly and spoke truthfully under trial, but Peter denied even knowing him.

On the orders of Pilate, at the request of the Jewish leaders, and in fulfillment of the Scriptures, Jesus was crucified and buried. His saving work was finished.

⊕ talkabout

1. Have you ever received some news that seemed too good to be true? What was it, and how did you respond?

⊕ investigate

> **Read John 20:30-31**

2. What does John say is the reason why he has written what he has written?

DICTIONARY

Signs (v 30): miracles.
Messiah (v 31): anointed one; the Old Testament promised the Messiah would rescue God's people.

This is the lens through which we should read the whole of John's Gospel, including his account of the greatest event ever known to man: the resurrection of Jesus Christ.

> **Read John 20:1-10**

DICTIONARY

Strips of linen (v 5): cloth used to wrap the body.

3. What do the following people find when they go to the tomb, and what conclusions do they come to?

• Mary

• Peter

• John ("the other disciple")

> **Read John 20:11-18**

DICTIONARY

Ascended to the Father (v 17): when Jesus would return to heaven in glory (see Acts 1:1-11).

4. "If it seems too good to be true, it usually is." How does Mary show something of that attitude in these verses?

5. Verse 16 is a beautiful moment. But why does Jesus tell Mary not to hold on to him (v 17)?

• What task does he give her?

▶ **Read John 20:19-23**

6. What words might you have expected the risen Jesus to first say to his disciples?

• Why is it significant that the first thing he says is "Peace be with you!"

7. What task does he give them?

Verse 23 is best understood as being connected to Jesus' commission in verse 21; in other words, the forgiving of people's sins is connected to the proclamation of the gospel of Jesus Christ. Any Spirit-empowered disciple of Jesus can preach the gospel of Jesus, and if someone comes to believe in Christ, we can declare that their sins are forgiven.

⮕ apply

The presence of Jesus gives peace and joy, and the commission of Jesus commands us to share this peace and joy by sharing him. Christians are sent people, not ghetto people. We are not people hiding from the world; we are sent into the world.

8. How has what you have read in this passage…

• reminded you of what the gospel message is?

• excited you about what the gospel message is?

9. Jesus' disciples were not expecting Jesus to come back to life. All of them had to be persuaded of it. How might this be helpful as we seek to engage with sceptical friends?

getting personal

Who do you want to share the truth of the resurrection with this week? Pray for one person you would like to speak to about what you've read.

explore more

optional

The bodily resurrection of Jesus Christ from the dead is unique—yet it ushers in a new era.

❯ Read Romans 8:29; 1 Corinthians 15:20-23; Colossians 1:18

What do these verses tell us about the meaning of the resurrection? How does this excite you, and give you confidence, about what will happen to you when you die?

investigate

Read John 20:24-29

DICTIONARY

Blessed (v 29): favored by God.

10. In what way is Jesus gracious to Thomas?

- In what way does Jesus challenge Thomas?

getting personal

"Stop doubting and believe." Are there areas of your life where you need to hear that challenge?

apply

11. John saw and believed (v 8). Thomas saw and believed (v 29). What surprising thing does Jesus say in verse 29?

- It is a more "blessed" situation to be reading the Bible than sitting outside the empty tomb on that first Easter Sunday or in the upper room a week later! How does that encourage you?

12. How has what you have read in John 20 helped you "believe that Jesus is the Messiah, the Son of God"?

- What would it look like for you to truly enjoy having "life in his name" this week?

↑ pray

- Worship Jesus as your Lord and your God.
- Thank God for John's resurrection account, and for giving us the Scriptures so that we may believe and have life.
- Pray for God's help to stop doubting and believe.
- Ask for the Holy Spirit's help to share the message of the risen Jesus with specific people you know.

8 John 21:1-25
BREAKFAST BY THE SEA

The story so far

With the help of Judas, the religious leaders arrested Jesus. Jesus went willingly and spoke truthfully under trial, but Peter denied even knowing him.

On the orders of Pilate, at the request of the Jewish leaders, and in fulfillment of the Scriptures, Jesus was crucified and buried. His saving work was finished.

On Sunday morning his friends found the tomb empty. The risen Jesus appeared to them and commissioned them to take the offer of life in his name to others.

⊕ talkabout

1. "The church is the only army that shoots its wounded." Do you agree? Why / why not?

How do you start again after you have failed? What does it take to find restoration and renewal? How can the church learn to restore, not shoot, its wounded? We find an answer to all of these questions in John 21.

⊙ investigate

> **Read John 21:1-14**

2. Describe the scene in verse 3. What do you think the disciples are thinking or feeling?

3. What do verses 4-6 tell us about Jesus? (See also v 12.)

- What do verses 7-9 tell us about Peter?

4. "Come and have breakfast," says Jesus in verse 12. Why is it significant that this is what Jesus chooses to do with his friends when he appears to them (v 1, 14)?

- What words would you use to describe the atmosphere at this breakfast?

→ **apply**

Jesus feeds his disciples. This breakfast on the beach is a physical picture of a spiritual reality.

5. What would it look like for you to "come and have breakfast" with Jesus?

6. Look at your answers to the second part of question 4. Have you experienced something similar in your fellowship with Jesus? Share specific examples.

⊎ investigate

> ▶ **Read John 21:15-23**

7. Jesus now addresses an "elephant in the room." What is it?

• Why does Jesus ask Peter if he loves him more than the other disciples do (v 15, see 13:37)?

• Why does Jesus ask Peter three times whether he loves him (v 17, see 18:15-18, 25-27)?

8. What does Jesus tell Peter to do (v 15, 16, 17)? What does he mean by this?

• What will it involve for Peter (v 18)?

optional

⊡ explore more

The heart of the pastoral office is feeding Christ's sheep.

❯ Read 2 Timothy 4:1-5

What does feeding the sheep involve? What might it cost?
What is the warning here for church members?
How should this passage, and John 21:15-23, shape our expectations of
our church leaders?

9. What do you think is behind Peter's question in verse 21? What do you
make of Jesus' reply?

⊡ getting personal

In what areas of life or ministry are you tempted to compare your lot
with those of others? Jesus says, "You must follow me" (v 22). How
will you take your eyes off other people, and keep them on Jesus?

⊡ apply

Jesus' words to Peter are particularly relevant to church leaders and
pastors, who have special responsibility as "under shepherds" of Christ's
flock (1 Peter 5:1-4). But every Christian is called to care for others.

10. In what particular areas are you called to "feed" and "take care of" the sheep?

- What difference will it make if you remember that other Christians are Jesus' sheep, not yours?

11. How can your church move toward being an army that restores its wounded, rather than shooting them? What would need to change?

- How might that play out in your personal relationships with one another?

⊡ **getting personal**

Have you done something in the past that still plagues your conscience? What do you need to take from this story of Peter's reinstatement?

⬇ investigate

> ❯ **Read John 21:24-25**

12. Think back over everything you've read in John's Gospel. What particular passages have encouraged you personally by showing you...

- the truth of the gospel (v 24)?

- the limitless character of Jesus (v 25)?

⬆ pray

Thank Jesus—the Good Shepherd—for the forgiveness and restoration he offers us when we fail.

Pray for your church family, that you would be increasingly gracious and gentle with the wounded.

Pray for your church leaders as they seek to feed and take care of Christ's sheep.

The place of
greatest glory
LEADER'S GUIDE

Leader's Guide

INTRODUCTION

Leading a Bible study can be a bit like herding cats—everyone has a different idea of what the passage could be about, and a different line of enquiry that they want to pursue. But a good group leader is more than someone who just referees this kind of discussion. You will want to:

- correctly understand and handle the Bible passage. But also…

- encourage and train the people in your group to do this for themselves. Don't fall into the trap of spoon-feeding people by simply passing on the information in the Leader's Guide. Then…

- make sure that no Bible study is finished without everyone knowing how the passage is relevant for them. What changes do you all need to make in the light of the things you have been learning? And finally…

- encourage the group to turn all that has been learned and discussed into prayer.

Your Bible-study group is unique, and you are likely to know better than anyone the capabilities, backgrounds and circumstances of the people you are leading. That's why we've designed these guides with a number of optional features. If they're a quiet bunch, you might want to spend longer on *talkabout*. If your time is limited, you can choose to skip *explore more*, or get people to look at these questions at home. Can't get enough of Bible study? Well, some studies have optional extra homework projects. As leader, you can adapt and select the material to the needs of your particular group.

So what's in the Leader's Guide?

The main thing that this Leader's Guide will help you to do is to understand the major teaching points in the passage you are studying, and how to apply them. As well as guidance for the questions, the Leader's Guide for each session contains the following important sections:

THE BIG IDEA

One or two key sentences will give you the main point of the session. This is what you should be aiming to have fixed in people's minds as they leave the Bible study. And it's the point you need to head back toward when the discussion goes off at a tangent.

SUMMARY

An overview of the passage, including plenty of useful historical background information.

OPTIONAL EXTRA

Usually this is an introductory activity that ties in with the main theme of the Bible study, and is designed to "break the ice" at the beginning of a session. Or it may be a "homework project" that people can tackle during the week.

So let's take a look at the various different features of a Good Book Guide:

⊕ talkabout

Each session kicks off with a discussion question, based on the group's opinions or experiences. It's designed to get people talking and thinking in a general way about the main subject of the Bible study.

⬇ investigate

The first thing you and your group need to know is what the Bible passage is about, which is the purpose of these questions. But watch out—people may come up with answers based on their experiences or teaching they have heard in the past, without referring to the passage at all. It's amazing how often we can get through a Bible study without actually looking at the Bible! If you're stuck for an answer, the Leader's Guide contains guidance for questions. These are the answers to direct your group to. This information isn't meant to be read out to people—ideally, you want them to discover these answers from the Bible for themselves. Sometimes there are optional follow-up questions (see ⊻ in guidance for questions) to help you help your group get to the answer.

☺ explore more

These questions generally point people to other relevant parts of the Bible. They are useful for helping your group to see how the passage fits into the "big picture" of the whole Bible. These sections are OPTIONAL—only use them if you have time. Remember that it's better to finish in good time having really grasped one big thing from the passage, than to try and cram everything in.

➔ apply

We want to encourage you to spend more time working at application—too often, it is simply tacked on at the end. In the Good Book Guides, apply sections are mixed in with the investigate sections of the study. We hope that people will realize that application is not just an optional extra, but rather, the whole purpose of studying the

Bible. We do Bible study so that our lives can be changed by what we hear from God's word. If you skip the application, the Bible study hasn't achieved its purpose.

These questions draw out practical lessons that we can all learn from the Bible passage. You can review what has been learned so far, and think about practical differences that this should make in our churches and our lives. The group gets the opportunity to talk about what they personally have learned.

☺ getting personal

These can be done at home, but it is well worth allowing a few moments of quiet reflection during the study for each person to think and pray about specific changes they need to make in their own lives. Why not have a time for reporting back at the beginning of the following session, so that everyone can be encouraged and challenged by one another to make application a priority?

⬆ pray

In Acts 4 v 25-30 the first Christians quoted Psalm 2 as they prayed in response to the persecution of the apostles by the Jewish religious leaders. Today however, it's not as common for Christians to base prayers on the truths of God's word as it once was. As a result, our prayers tend to be weak, superficial and self-centered rather than bold, visionary and God-centered.

The prayer section is based on what has been learned from the Bible passage. How different our prayer times would be if we were genuinely responding to what God has said to us through his word.

1 John 13:1-38
POWER TO SERVE

THE BIG IDEA
Christ shows his love for his people by laying down his power and serving them—and he calls his people to love one another in the same way.

SUMMARY
Sometimes it seems as if everything is about power—even religion. But Jesus is so different, because he is love, as this passage shows.

Verse 1 begins with a time marker: "It was just before the Passover." John's readers knew that Jesus had died on the cross at Passover, as do we today, and so John here turns our minds away from the immediate to that event which this event foreshadows. 13:1-17, which describes the famous foot-washing scene in the upper room, is intended to teach us two key things: first, that Jesus served, and that we are meant to be serving people too (v 14-17); second, that Jesus' love is revealed in his serving actions, ultimately at the cross—"he loved [his disciples] to the end" (v 1). The cross would be the means by which he makes his people clean (v 10-11).

God's sovereign control is another major theme. Jesus took to his knees to wash his disciples' feet as a consequence of knowing that "the Father had put all things under his power" (v 3). He had clear foreknowledge both of Judas' betrayal (v 18-30) and Peter's denial (v 31-38). He shared this foreknowledge with his disciples: "... so that when it does happen you will believe that I am who I am" (v 19)—the Messiah, and the Son of God (see John's purpose statement in

writing his Gospel in 20:31). The events that were about to follow were not a surprise or a detour for Jesus, but an essential part of God's sovereign salvation plan—because it was at the cross that Jesus would be most glorified as his sacrificial love was put on display (13:13-32).

OPTIONAL EXTRA
Before the study, give each member of your group a section of John 1 – 12 to read, and ask them to come prepared with a one-sentence summary of what happens, and what that tells us about Jesus. Have each person report back to the group in order, so as to build up a picture of where we've got to in John's Gospel already.

GUIDANCE FOR QUESTIONS
1. Have you ever seen someone in a position of power do something unexpected? What was it, and what made it so surprising? The aim of this question is to get your group thinking about power, and the type of things we expect (and don't expect) powerful people to do. If you have time, you could probe people to explore the type of reactions these incidents provoked. Were people touched or unnerved to see a powerful person acting "out of role"? No matter how familiar we are with the story of Jesus washing his disciples feet, we shouldn't lose the shock of seeing the Lord of the universe stoop to the role of a servant.

2. What is it that is moving Jesus both to go to the cross and to wash his disciples' feet (v 1)? Why is this

extraordinary? Jesus is moved by love. The purpose of this foot-washing is to point us to the ultimate place where love is shown—the cross. How were the disciples to understand why Jesus was going to die on the cross, as they made their journey ever closer to Passover? Jesus takes off his outer clothing and picks up a basin and a towel and teaches them about the nature of salvation, of victory, of love, of sacrifice, and of service. The washing of the disciples' feet is not an ordinance or a sacrament; it is a metaphor, a sign, pointing to the love of Jesus at the end, at the cross.

3. Look at the way John describes this moment in verses 3-5. What is so shocking about what Jesus does? John 13:3 tells us that Jesus knew that God the Father had put all things under his power, that he had come from God, and that he was returning to God. Yet a remarkable event occurs in verse 4: "... *so* he got up from the meal, took off his outer clothing, and wrapped a towel around his waist." Can you imagine the surprised looks as in the middle of the meal Jesus takes on the mantle of a servant? In ancient times, feet were dirty. People walked in sandals in open streets covered with dung from animals as well as the dust from wayfarers. It deserves significant reflection and imagination to picture those hands that flung the stars into outer space now grappling with the corns around the disciples' feet, wiping off the droppings of some goat, smearing out the filth, and then, when all is clean, studiously and carefully wiping the feet dry.

4. Why does Peter object to having his feet washed, do you think (v 6-8)? What has he misunderstood about Jesus? You should feel the force of Peter's astonishment as you read his question in verse 6. Peter

objects to anything that might humiliate Jesus or undermine his dignity. He wants Jesus to be lifted up, not brought down to washing people's feet. Jesus points to the meaning of this event by replying in verse 7, "You do not realize now what I am doing, but later you will understand." When his disciples stand at the foot of the cross, and when the Spirit reveals to them the meaning of the cross, they will understand that they worship a crucified Messiah, a serving Lord, a loving and humble God.

- **What is it that makes him change his mind (v 8-9)? What has he rightly understood about Jesus?** Jesus' reply in verse 8 makes Peter change his mind: "Unless I wash you, you have no part with me." Peter rightly understands how important it is to be identified with Jesus. Peter may have made many mistakes, but what sets him out is his simple, clear, pure desire to please Jesus come what may. Let us have that desire!

5. In what way is this footwashing...
- **a picture of the love Christ will show on the cross (v 10-11)?** He came to serve, and in this incident he begins to show the full extent of his love—or the end point of his love—which will be ultimately shown in the cross. There is no other way to heaven but through the basin and the towel of Jesus' sacrifice for us (v 10). But, as Peter shows us, how hard it is for a sinner to learn to accept they need a Savior! Surely there is something complicated we must do. Surely we must work hard and prove ourselves to God. No—it begins with and requires only the humility to allow Jesus to wash us.

- **an example of the love he expects his people to demonstrate (v 12-15)?** Jesus is showing them that authority and power should not be used to our own advantage, but laid down in loving, humbling, service of others: "I have set you an example that you should do as I have done for you" (v 15). Real love serves.

6. APPLY: Think about some of the things you do for others at church, home or work. How can we tell whether our actions are genuine acts of service? A large part of it is attitude. Are we hoping to be noticed or appreciated, or are we simply looking to serve out of love?

7. APPLY: What two motivations does Jesus give for us to serve others in this way (v 16-17)?
• **How will these help you to be increasingly servant-hearted?**
First, being a servant establishes that we are in relationship with God (v 16). It gives us assurance. We bear the Master's image when we act like a servant. What an upside down world is the kingdom of God! Second, Jesus promises that if we serve others, we will be blessed (v 17): happy, joyful, in a state of what Jesus declares is the right way to live—even when you don't feel like it. You enter into his blessing, even in the shadow of the cross. We will not feel the need to seek the approval or praise of others if we remember that our actions bring pleasure to our heavenly Father.

8. Why does Jesus tell his disciples that he is going to be betrayed (v 19)? Jesus is telling his disciples about Judas so that when the betrayal happens, they will believe that Jesus is who he says he is ("that I am who I am"): that is, that he is the Messiah, the Son of God (see 20:31). Only God can predict such an event; even the betrayal is under God's control. If Jesus didn't warn his friends, they might think that Jesus

had somehow been taken by surprise or overpowered. Nothing could be further from the truth.

9. How does this incident show God's total sovereign control over the events that are about to unfold?
• **Verse 18:** Jesus' betrayal fulfills prophecy spoken hundreds of years before.
• **Verse 21:** Jesus shows that he knows that one of his own disciples—his closest friends—is going to betray him.
• **Verse 26:** Jesus knows it will be Judas specifically.
• **Verse 27:** Jesus tells Judas not to delay but to get on with it. Bad things do not become better by stretching them out. Jesus is willing to be betrayed because he knows it is part of God's sovereign salvation plan.

EXPLORE MORE
What does Peter warn Christians about [in 1 Peter 5:8-11]? He warns us that the devil is prowling around like a lion, looking for someone to devour. Satan will do everything he can to derail our faith.
Do you give much thought to this prowling lion? In Western culture, the answer is probably no. **Why is that, do you think?** By and large, our culture dismisses the idea of a real, personal force of evil. The devil is regarded as a fictional creature, good only for inspiring scary movies. Christians in other cultures have a greater awareness of demonic powers. While it is possible, and unhelpful, to have too great an emphasis on this, it would seem that Western Christians have probably swung too far the other way.
What does Peter tell us to do? We are to "be alert and of sober mind" (v 8). Do not play with evil things; there is a devil, and

there are evil spirits. The occult, witchcraft and Satan are not to be toyed with. We should not see the devil behind every closet or underneath every carpet, or as the prompting for all unpleasantness, but neither should we ignore his malevolent work. The devil is real. He is roaring around looking for someone to devour. We are to stand firm in our faith, resisting him, and he will flee from us (see James 4:7).

10. Where and how will God's glory be most clearly displayed (v 31-32)?

The glory of God is shown nowhere more intensely than in the cross of Jesus. These verses comes between Judas' plans to betray Jesus (v 29-30) and Peter beginning the path to denying him (v 36-38). This is, surprisingly, God's glory! Jesus' death will lead us to wonder at the glory of God shown in such humility in such a Savior.

- **How is this different to the way we normally think about glory?** God is most glorified in the sufferings and death of Jesus. We tend to be triumphalistic and think that God's glory is shown in our successes. But could it be that, instead, his glory is shown more in our sufferings? When we are weak, then we are strong (2 Corinthians 12:10).

11. Jesus has clear foreknowledge of both Judas' betrayal and Peter's denial. How does this make his earlier foot-washing even more remarkable? This

question is an opportunity to draw together the key themes of this study: Jesus had complete power and authority—so much so that he saw past his friends' appearance of loyalty to what would really happen (Judas' betrayal on the one hand, and Peter's outright denial on the other). And yet he chose to wash their feet anyway. What humility! That is how much Jesus loves

Peter—he is willing to die for him, even though Peter will be unwilling to do likewise.

12. APPLY: To what extent is your church characterized by this kind of love [in John 13:34-35]? We are the church, the

family of God. And we are to show that by the love we have for each other (v 35). It is to be what sets us apart. The theologian Tertullian saw how the Christians being persecuted by the Roman Empire fulfilled this command when the pagans said of the Christians, "Look how they love one another." Are we the kind of people of whom the non-Christians around us would say—even begrudgingly, while disagreeing with what we believe—that those are people who love each other? Encourage your group to appraise your church's culture, without pointing the finger of blame at individuals.

- **Instead of love, what other things are you in danger of prizing most dearly as a church?** Could it be that you are more characterized by bickering over amendments to bylaws and constitutions? Are your congregational meetings or parish councils marked by such love, or by a worldly suspicion of motives? It might be that you are so attached to your programs and policies, or so focused on issues of right doctrine, that you are missing the key ingredient: love.

- **What would it look like for you to move closer to the vision that Jesus has for his church?** Push your group to be specific. For example, love the annoying person next to you at church. Love the person who sings loudly and flat. Love the person whose breath smells. Love the person whose social dexterity is borderline weird. Love the person who sins, even when the sin is against you (without loving the sin; hate that). Love one another. This doctrine of Christ is proved by the love of Christians. This all goes back to 13:1. This discussion will likely show where you have all fallen short; let that move you to earnest prayer at the end of this session, and to rejoice that it is Jesus who washes us clean and offers forgiveness for our lack of love.

2 John 14:1-31
PROMISES FOR TROUBLED HEARTS

THE BIG IDEA

Jesus is the way, the truth and the life—he alone can comfort his disciples with the promise of a place in his presence in heaven in the future, and with the promise of his ongoing presence through the Holy Spirit today.

SUMMARY

When the disciples are told by Jesus at the end of chapter 13 that he is about to leave them, understandably they are disturbed. It is not clear to them where he is going, or why it is that they cannot follow him (13:36, 37). In chapters 14 to 17, therefore, Jesus gives them comfort. Not comfort in the sense of sentimentality, but in the old sense of the word—courage and conviction and personal power to overcome difficulties, through the promise of heaven and the work of the Holy Spirit. This study takes in chapter 14 in three sections:

• Verses 1-4: Jesus says that he is going to prepare a place for his disciples in his "Father's house" (heaven). One day they will come to be with him.

• Verses 5-14: The disciples do not understand. Thomas asks, *How can we know the way to where you are going*

when we don't even know where you are going?! Jesus patiently replies with words that are justly famous and thoroughly essential in our relativistic age: "I am the way and the truth and the life. No one comes to the Father except through me" (v 6). Jesus is making a strong case for his identity as God (v 7). Again, the disciples do not understand (v 8). Jesus says that if you've seen him, you've seen the Father. So Jesus asks Philip, and the other disciples, and by extension now us, to believe in him (v 11), and promises that those who do will be part of something "great"—the evangelization of the world (v 12).

• Verses 15-31: In verse 16 we are introduced to a special word for the Spirit: the "Advocate" (also in 14:26; 15:26; 16:7). The Spirit will bring the disciples the presence, the truth, and the peace of God. Jesus also emphasizes love and obedience. The Son loved the Father and so obeyed him (v 31). And, says Jesus, by the help of the Spirit he will send, his people are to love him by displaying toward him that same joyful, trusting, sacrificial obedience.

OPTIONAL EXTRA

In chapters 14 to 17 Jesus gives his disciples comfort in the face of his impending death. To introduce your group to a biblical definition of "comfort" (as opposed to a more modern one), find a picture online of the panel from the Bayeux Tapestry captioned "Bishop Odo comforts the troops." Ask your group if they know what the Bayeux Tapestry is (it depicts the invasion of England by William the Conqueror of Normandy in 1066), and what they think is going on in this picture. Then tell them what the caption says: "ODO ERS: BACVLV. TENENS: CONFOR:-TAT PVEROS" (in Latin) or "Bishop Odo, holding a club, rallies [comforts] the young troops." Odo was a Norman bishop and the half-brother of William the Conqueror. In what sense is Odo "comforting" the troops? What does this tell us about what this word means? Explain that this is the kind of comfort that Jesus promises his disciples in this passage.

GUIDANCE FOR QUESTIONS

1. Can you think of a time when a respected leader announced they were leaving? How did it feel? What kinds of things helped to smooth the transition in leadership? When someone we love, respect and wish to emulate leaves us, we naturally feel bereft and disappointed. Transition can be helped by the leader preparing the team, rather than leaving unexpectedly; the team all pulling in the same direction, with a clear sense of what they are meant to be doing; or, a new leader being found quickly. In this passage Jesus is preparing his disciples for his departure. This won't be a change in leadership per se—from now on Jesus will be with his disciples through the Holy Spirit, but not physically.

2. How does Jesus expect his disciples to be feeling at this moment (v 1)? He anticipates that they are feeling "troubled." **Why might they be feeling this way?** Departures are hard at the best of times. So when these disciples are told by Jesus at the end of chapter 13 that he is about to leave them, understandably they are discomforted and disturbed. It is not clear to them where he is going, or why it is that they cannot follow him (13:36, 37). In chapters 14 to 17, therefore, Jesus gives them comfort.

3. What promise does Jesus make to comfort them? Jesus says that he is going to prepare a place for them in his Father's house.

- **What is he talking about? Why does he choose this image, do you think?** Jesus is talking about heaven. There are many layers of significance to the house metaphor. Home is a place of intimacy and security. There are also "many rooms." That is, there is a specific, personally designed place for you individually. So valuable does Jesus consider us that he prepares a place specifically for each of us in heaven.

- **What will it take for Jesus to "prepare a place" in heaven for the disciples?** Jesus is talking here about the power of the cross to win heaven for us. Since Jesus went to all this painful, bloody effort, then surely he will do the relatively simple thing of actually taking us to be with him in the heaven. Therefore, "do not let your hearts be troubled."

4. Jesus makes a big claim in response to Thomas's question. What is it (v 6)? That he is the way, the truth, and the life. No one comes to the Father except through him.

- **What are some of the implications of this claim?** Encourage your group to really drill down into the details of this verse. Jesus does not merely show us the way, teach us the truth, and give us an example of how to live. Because Jesus is the Word eternal (John 1:1), he *is* the way, truth and life. He himself embodies what it is to be alive and what it is to know truth, and he is the very way to heaven itself. But not only is Jesus positively the way, the truth and the life; negatively, "No one comes to the Father except through me" (14:6). No one—not some people in some situation at some times, but no one whatsoever and completely—can come to the Father except through faith in Jesus.

5. How would you sum up what Jesus says in verses 7-11 in one sentence? *If you've seen Jesus, you've seen the Father.* Here Jesus is emphasizing his divinity and his unity with the Father.

• **What is the link between this and what Jesus has just said in verses 1-6?** Jesus promises his friends a place in heaven (v 1-4); he can make that promise because he is the way to the Father (v 6); and he is the way to the Father because he is God—as the Son, he is in intimate communion with the Father.

6. APPLY: What is it about verse 6 that is so controversial in our culture today? Have you come across this attitude in your own experience? Many a person has attempted to downplay, bowdlerize, dilute, or even deny what Jesus says here. Today, religious pluralism means that Christ's claims here are considered to be intolerant, exclusive or bigoted.

• **What is the good news in verse 6? How can we make sure we communicate that positively?** There is a way to the Father! If we come through

Jesus, we can be certain that God will accept us. There is such a thing as absolute truth—there's no need to feel adrift in a sea of moral relativism, uncertain of what to believe. Jesus shows us what is true and real. And while we must all come face to face with the frightening inevitability of death, Jesus can offer us the hope of eternal life. This is good news indeed!

7. APPLY: What truths do you see in these verses that motivate you toward more urgent evangelism? Allow your group to share what has impacted them personally. It might be the goodness of Jesus' promise in verses 1-4; the fact that there is no other way to be saved except through Jesus (v 6); that Jesus shows us the Father (which challenges Muslim and Unitarian views of God, v 10). Draw your group's attention to verse 12: when we are sharing the gospel, we are part of something that Jesus declared was an even greater thing than what he did. Surely that should motivate us to evangelism!

8. What do the following verses tell us about the Holy Spirit:
• **v 16:** "Advocate" (also used in verse 26) has the idea of a "helper" or "intercessor" who comes to a person's aid in a court of law—a role that Jesus himself also fulfills ("he will give you *another* advocate"). Note that the Holy Spirit is the gift of God the Father, given at the request of Jesus the Son. He will be with us "forever." How comforting it is that the advocate will not be taken away from us!

• **v 17a:** God's Spirit leads us into truth and is the truth. There is no false antithesis between knowledge and experience here; to have the Spirit is to have the Spirit of truth, and where the Spirit is at work, Christians desire to learn more of the truth.

- **v 17b:** The Spirit cannot be physically seen, so it will be normal for people who are not Christians ("the world") to reject the notion of the work of the Spirit. But if we believe in and follow Jesus, then we will have the Spirit in us, and we will know his work and know him ourselves.

- **v 18:** Jesus will not leave his disciples as "orphans" (v 18), alone and without fatherly protection and care; he will "come" to them (either by his resurrection or by the gift of the Spirit—what he means in this verse is not entirely clear). One of the great truths of the gospel to enjoy today is that the Christian is never alone. God is with those who believe by his Spirit.

- **v 26:** Jesus promises that the Holy Spirit will come from the Father in the name of the Son, and that when he comes, he will "teach [the disciples] all things and will remind you of everything I have said to you." Jesus is promising the special work of the Spirit to inspire the apostles to author the New Testament (as in 16:13).

9. What link does Jesus draw between love and obedience (v 15, v 21, v 23-24)?

If we love Jesus, we will obey him (v 15). Conversely, if someone does not love him, they will not obey his teaching (v 24). In verse 21 Jesus adds that a result of loving obedience is that his disciples will experience Jesus' love and know more of Jesus too. Jesus is not saying that we are saved by our own good works. He is saying that a real Christian will show his or her love for God by obedience, and that such a life is one which enjoys the experience of God's love. If God seems distant, it is worth examining ourselves to see whether there is some area of disobedience where we need to come into line with God's word.

- **Is that normally how we think? Why / why not?** We tend to think of obedience as semi-legalistic, and love as overtly sentimental. But for Jesus, if we love him, we will obey him. As he is the incarnate Son of God, to love him means to bow before him. Note that the way to grow in your obedience of Jesus is to grow in your love for Jesus. The more you love him, the more you will obey him.

- **How does Jesus model perfect loving obedience to his Father (v 30-31)?** The Son loved the Father, and so obeyed him by going to the cross. And, says Jesus, by the help of the Spirit, his people are to love him by displaying that same joyful, trusting, sacrificial obedience.

10. In verse 27 Jesus says for a second time, "Do not let your hearts be troubled" (see also v 1). How would you summarize…
- **the reasons he has given his disciples to not be troubled?**
- **the authority with which he makes those statements?**

This is an opportunity for you to make sure you group has grasped the big idea of this study: Jesus comforts his disciples with the promise of a place in his presence in heaven in the future, and with the promise of his ongoing presence through the Holy Spirit today. He makes those promises, and can deliver on those promises, because he is "the way and the truth and the life" (v 6).

EXPLORE MORE
What do these verses [John 1:1-2, 5:19-20, 6:38, 10:30, 14:11, 14:28, 14:31] reveal about the relationship of the Father and the Son? If you're pressed for time, you could split your group into pairs and get them to look at one of the verses each. Jesus is the eternal word of God—he

is not a created being (1:1-2); Father and Son work in perfect unity and love (5:19-20); the Son is sent by the Father and does his will (6:38); the Son and the Father are one—they are equal in divine power and nature (10:30); the Son reveals the Father (14:11); the Father is "greater than" the Son (14:28); and the Son lovingly submits to the Father (14:31). One of the most difficult ideas for 21st-century Western minds to grasp is that submission to someone does not mean a diminishment of your own identity. You can be fully equal with someone and yet submit to them, for you can have different roles from them. This submission is modeled by the Trinity: the Son submits to the Father as "greater" than him. This is not to say that Jesus is in any way "less" than the Father in identity or power or personhood. Yet he submits to the Father, willingly and lovingly. The Father, Son and Holy Spirit, while equal, all have different roles.

How does this move you to worship the triune God more deeply? In the Trinity we see perfect love, equality and unity—what a God to worship! No matter how much time and thought we give to this (and throughout church history, great minds have devoted plenty of both to the doctrine of the Trinity), we will always be left standing in awe and wonder at the God who is above and beyond anything we could imagine.

11. APPLY: Since the apostles were inspired by the Spirit to write the New Testament, what implications does that have for how we approach the Bible? The primary application of these verses for Christians today is to be grateful for the Bible, to read the Bible, and to hear from the Bible. The secondary application, though, is the way in which the Spirit helps us with understanding the Bible. If we are ever stuck understanding something in the Bible, we

can ask God by his Spirit to open our eyes that we may see wondrous things in his word—and we can be confident that all that we need to understand, he will lead us to understand.

- **When have you experienced the Spirit giving you comfort in troubled times through the pages of Scripture?** Encourage your group to share specific verses and truths that the Spirit has impressed upon them in the midst of difficult circumstances. Use these testimonies as the basis for thanksgiving as you close your session in prayer.

3 John 15:1 – 16:33
FRUIT THAT WILL LAST

THE BIG IDEA
Jesus calls us to remain in him, the true vine—although this will put us at odds with the world, he will cause us to bear the fruit of love and joy.

SUMMARY
It is the night before he dies, and Jesus is preparing his disciples for life after he has risen and ascended to heaven. Forewarned is forearmed (16:33).

First, Jesus tells them to remain in him (15:1-17). Just as a branch is connected to the vine and relies on it for everything, so the disciples are connected to Jesus and rely on him to bear the fruit of love and Christ-like character.

Second, Jesus warns the disciples that belonging to him will put them at odds with "the world" (all those in rebellion against God) (v 18-25). The world hates Jesus, so they will hate Jesus' people.

But Jesus promises the disciples what they will need to withstand the assault: the Holy Spirit (15:26 – 16:15). He will enable the apostles to testify about Jesus (15:26-27) and to author the New Testament (16:12-15). The Spirit will bring some hearers to conviction and repentance through the apostles' message (v 8-11). So valuable and powerful is the indwelling of the Holy Spirit that Jesus says it is "for [the disciples'] good" that he is going away, as it facilitates the Spirit's sending (v 7).

Finally, in 16:16, Jesus tells his disciples, "In a little while you will see me no more, and then after a little while you will see me," referring to his death and resurrection.

Although the next 48 hours will be distressing, as the disciples are scattered and abandon Jesus at his arrest (v 32), Jesus promises that joy is coming—just as a new mother rejoices at the birth of her child (v 20-22). Ultimately, Jesus is "leaving the world and going back to the Father" (v 28). But he leaves the disciples with the assurance of his love, the promise of peace, and the presence of the Holy Spirit. Therefore, "take heart!" (v 33).

OPTIONAL EXTRA
Have an extended time of prayer for persecuted Christians. To help you, ask a group member to download some information and prayer points from an organization such as Open Doors (opendoors.org). At the end of your study, pray that these brothers and sisters would respond to the world's hatred with love and joy as they remain in Christ.

GUIDANCE FOR QUESTIONS
1. What is the key to being fruitful at work? What about in the Christian life?
A basic human desire is to be productive. We wish to "bear fruit" in some way or other: in children, career, influence, finances, territory. Normally the key to "bearing fruit" at work is to work hard, to focus, to maintain good working relationships or make strategic decisions, and so on. While there is this basic human desire to bear fruit, there is also a specific Christian desire too. We wish to honor Jesus, to see his kingdom expand, to be fruitful in character and in church health and growth, in conversions and Christ-likeness. What is the way to bear much fruit? Jesus' teaching here in

this section addresses that question—and it stands in contrast to the way we think about fruitfulness in other areas of life.

2. What is meant by each of the elements in this metaphor?

- **The vine (v 1)** is Jesus.
- **The gardener (v 1)** is the Father. He is the one who takes care of the vine and prunes it and nurtures it.
- **The branches (v 5)** are the disciples—Christians, including us. We are not the vine! The vine is Jesus. The picture of our subsidiary relationship to Christ ought to begin to shift our sense of how it is that we produce fruit.
- **The fruit (v 5, 8; look at what Jesus goes on to talk about in particular in verses 9-17)** 15:9-17 shows that, in the first instance, the "fruit" is Christ-like character in the lives of believers. There will be some love, joy, patience, or kindness. No Christian is perfect, but a real Christian bears some fruit.

3. What does Jesus say is key to being fruitful as a Christian?

- **v 2:** It is interesting that Jesus immediately pushes the picture to a painful place—the Father will "prune" branches so that they bear more fruit. Circumstances, difficulties, trials, opposition, suffering—all will be used to bring about greater Christ-likeness.
- **v 4-5:** The key to fruitfulness is this "remaining" in Christ. Prayer, fasting, quiet times, God's word—all these ways to "remain" are the ways to be fruitful. We do "nothing" spiritually fruitful apart from Christ. Although our Lord frequently has mercy on our prayerlessness and sinfulness, there is still a straight line between remaining in him and fruitfulness.

- **v 7-8:** Prayer is key. The more we get to know Christ, the more we want what Christ wants, and therefore the more effective are our prayers (because when we pray what we want, we are increasingly praying what he wants). Verse 8 reminds us that the goal of growing in Christ-like character is never to make ourselves look good—it is something we strive for in order to glorify God.
- **v 9-11:** As God loves Christ, so Christ loves us. The call to us is to remain in that love. Christians of all people are to be known for their love for God, for each other, and for their neighbors. That love (as we have seen, 14:21) is expressed in moral obedience. And the purpose of all this is joy (16:11)!
- **v 16:** When all the expectations of being a Christian can seem overwhelming, we do well to remember this verse. Our choice of God is always secondary to God's choice of us. This should humble us and encourage us. Underneath our waverings are always the eternal loving arms of the Father. What is more, the desire that we have to be fruitful and productive for Christ was first Christ's desire for us!

4. APPLY: How is what Jesus says in these verses...

- **a relief?** It is a relief to remember who the vine is (it's not us); and to remember who causes the growth (it's not us). Paradoxically, all spiritual fruitfulness begins with a sense that the productivity we desire is outside of our control. Jesus is the true vine. The Father is the gardener. What a relief to know we're not responsible for meeting targets or driving strategies—all we have to do is cling on to Jesus as we remain in him.
- **a warning?** A real Christian bears some

fruit. If there is no fruit at all, then the Father will bring to light the pretense and take away that pseudo-branch (v 2). Do not take lightly your relationship with God. Whether such a "branch" that is "thrown away" was ever really truly a Christian or not is, to some extent, beside the point. The warning of verse 6 still stands. You can paper over the cracks for a while, sometimes for years; and God is merciful toward our multitude of weaknesses. But it does not deny the principle: apart from him you can do nothing.

• **something to be excited about?**
Through us, God is doing something incredibly exciting—he is growing fruit that will last! It would be worth drawing your group's attention to verses 14-15. Jesus is saying that if we obey his commands, we have this deeply connected relationship of intimacy with him. We are not merely ordered around like slaves; we are now "called … friends". We are "in the know," included in the plans, able to hear what it is that God wants from us and for us.

5. What kind of reaction can the disciples expect from "the world" (15:18, 16:2)? The "world" in John is the human order of society, and its individual human members, that is in rebellion against God (even those who outwardly look religious or self-righteous). They will hate Christ's people, and even try to harm them. **Why (15:19-25)?** Animosity toward us is not really personal—it is an animosity against Christ himself. The world do not want God; therefore, they do not want God's Son (v 21, 24). Jesus "chose" us out of this world. We are his. And "that is why" the world hates us (v 19). Some sort of opposition, at some point or other in our lives, is the necessary corollary of being a Christ-follower, chosen by Christ.

Note: In what sense would someone not be "guilty of sin" if they don't hear about Jesus (15:22, 24)? Jesus is not saying that people live in a state of original innocence. If it is necessary for the world to be rescued (see 3:16), that is because it is sinful. But there's a way in which evangelization clarifies the issues. If someone, having heard the gospel, still rejects Jesus, then it is made abundantly clear that they are in opposition to God. In fact, the gospel not only therefore saves; it also condemns those who reject it: "Now they have no excuse for their sin" (15:22, see also 2 Corinthians 2:16).

EXPLORE MORE
Why does Jesus choose to identify himself with this Old Testament King [David] by quoting [Psalm 35 and Psalm 69] in John 15:25, do you think? In John 15:25 the word "law" simply means the "Old Testament." It is "their" (the Jews') law, because it is that which they rely upon—but it is that very law that speaks of Jesus and convicts them of their sin in rejecting him. In referencing these psalms, Jesus is aligning himself with David—he is great David's greater Son, the Messiah in David's line. As they rejected David without cause, so much more will they reject the Messiah himself. Even Jesus' rejection is under God's sovereign plan.

6. What are the disciples called to do in the face of this opposition (15:26 – 16:15)? They are to testify about Jesus as they preach and teach in the power of the Holy Spirit. In 16:13 Jesus promises that his apostles, the core team of disciples, will, by the Spirit, be inspired to author the New Testament.

7. What else does Jesus promise in order to help them (15:26-27; 16:7-15)?

An "advocate". The Spirit's role is to bring conviction to the world (16:7-11). He stirs in people a sense that things are not as they should be, that their lives are not as they were meant to be, and that there is some accounting still to come (see Explore More below for further questions on these verses). Notice what a high value Jesus places on the Spirit in verse 7—when Jesus goes he will send the Spirit, and in this sense it is "for your good that [Jesus] is going away". There surely were benefits to being with Jesus physically, but the believer now has something better—God's Spirit in them!

8. Why is Jesus telling his disciples these things (16:1)? Jesus is teaching this to his disciples "so that you will not fall away" (16:1). The disciples will be in real spiritual danger, not merely physical danger. Forewarned is forearmed.

EXPLORE MORE
What is the Spirit's role in the world (v 8)? The Spirit's role is to "prove the world to be in the wrong." That is, the Spirit is to show, by prodding the consciences of people, that there is such a thing as sin, and that they are failing to avoid sinning; that there is such a thing as righteousness, a standard that they do not meet; and that there is a judgment to come for such failure to attain the standard required by the Holy God himself. When the Spirit moves with power, this is what he does: he convicts of sin. A mourning over sin that leads to repentance is therefore one of the sure signs of the Spirit's work.

In order to be saved, what is it that we must understand about...
- **sin (v 9)?** The Spirit is given to convict of sin. Note Jesus does not say here that the role of the Spirit is to give faith (though see Ephesians 2:8), but to convict of sin

where there is no faith. Faith, then, is a response to a profound sense of need. It is a trusting cry to Jesus to be saved. A man on dry land may in a certain sense believe in a lifeboat. But he does not trust his life to a lifeboat until he finds himself drowning at sea.
- **righteousness (v 10)?** People are looking for the right standard to live by. What is the right way to live? When Jesus was in the world, the answer to that was simple, if uncomfortable: be like Jesus. Now, without Jesus physically present, that standard of righteousness is one step removed. The Spirit's role is to fill this "gap"; he will convict the world of the righteous standard contained in Jesus' teachings and life, which people do not keep.
- **judgment (v 11)?** The "prince of this world"— Satan—is cast out and defeated by the work of Christ. Christ refutes Satan's false teaching and lies. He defeats death itself. In the gospel, the rule of Christ is declared to release captives from prison, set free the sinner, and save the guilty. One day that rule of Christ (his judgment) will be made forever manifest on the day of judgment. In all this the Holy Spirit has the task of showing, empowering, furthering, enabling, and convicting.

How should these verses...
- **shape what we pray about for our non-Christian friends?** We should be praying that the Spirit would be convicting them in these three key areas, causing them to cry out to Jesus for rescue.
- **shape what we say to our non-Christian friends?** We might explore questions such as these: Do you sense that something is not right with the world? What do you think the problem is? Are you the person you want to be? Have you ever seriously looked at the life of Jesus?

What do you think happens when we die? In all these conversations we are seeking to testify to the truth about Jesus—and we pray that through our words the Spirit would bring conviction.

9. What does Jesus say is going to happen soon (v 16)? What does he mean by this? Jesus will leave them to die on the cross. But then he will be raised again, and they will see him. Then he will depart as he ascends to heaven. But then he will send his Spirit to be with them. And then, finally, he will return on the last day. Verse 16 puts a time stamp on, and introduces a note of urgency to, the whole discourse. They only have a certain amount of time left to hear from Jesus everything they need to hear.

10. What does Jesus say about joy in verses 19-24? Why do you think he chooses to say this to his disciples now? Jesus' clarification for his disciples here is that the timescale of their joy needs to be adjusted (v 20). We should not judge the purposes of God by our usual timescales. His point with the childbirth analogy is not that our pain in this world is not real or valid (giving birth really is painful!). But in the same way that holding a child outweighs the experience of suffering in childbirth, so the knowledge of the love of Christ outweighs the sufferings that we experience in this world as we follow him. But Jesus is not only talking about heaven here; he is talking about when the disciples will see him "again", meaning after his resurrection from the dead (v 22). Pain is coming… but so is joy.

11. Look at verses 25-33. How does what Jesus says here re-emphasise some of the things we've already seen

in John 13 – 16? Repeated themes include asking for things in Jesus' name (v 26; see 14:14); the Father's love for Christ's people (16:27; see 14:23); Jesus' return to the Father (16:28; see 13:1); the importance of believing that Jesus has come from God (16:30, see 14:10); the disciple's impending abandonment of Jesus (16:32, see 13:38); that Jesus gives his followers peace (16:33, see 14:27); the need to take heart instead of feeling troubled (16:33, see 14:1, 27).

12. APPLY: Have you experienced hatred for being a disciple of Jesus? If so, what did it look like? Encourage one or two members of your group to share examples from their own life. We cannot duck the implications that all faithful Christians should experience some degree of opposition, but we should be careful to contextualize the nature of that opposition. In a society that still accepts (however loosely) a Judeo-Christian worldview, opposition to Christians will be more muted. When the world-system has the levers of governmental authority, then prison and jail and even lethal attack can be the forms which opposition takes.

• **What truths from this passage will we need to remind ourselves of next time we face opposition from the world?** Allow your group to share the things that have struck them from this passage, while seeking to draw together everything we've covered. Jesus is with us by his Spirit. The world hates us because we belong to him, the true vine. However hard things are, the most important thing is to remain in him, so that we grow in Christ-like character even in the midst of opposition.

4 John 17:1-26
A TIME FOR GLORY

THE BIG IDEA

Jesus models how to pray. His prayer focuses on his disciples' spiritual protection, sanctification, unity, and love, for the glory of God.

SUMMARY

Prayer is something that it is easier to talk about than to do. But John 17 shows us Jesus praying. He practices what he preaches. In this passage we find not just a lesson about prayer but a model of prayer.

In the first part of the prayer, Jesus is praying for himself (v 1-5). The burden of these verses is the glory of God and of the Son. The "hour" has come for Jesus to "finish" the work he has been sent to do—the place of his greatest glory is the blood-stained cross and the empty tomb.

Second, Jesus prays for his disciples (v 6-19)—those who have been given to him and have accepted the truth he has taught. As Jesus will soon be leaving the world, he prays for their spiritual protection (v 11-12), joy (v 13), and sanctification (v 17). This too is all for God's glory (v 10).

Finally, Jesus prays for not-yet Christians who will come to faith through the disciples' message. He prays "that all of them may be one" (v 21). Church unity is a powerful testimony to the truth of the gospel (v 23). Jesus' desire is that we might see his glory and know his love (v 26).

How wonderful to know that these are what Jesus wants for us—the challenge for us is to pray with these same priorities. This study is shorter than normal to give you plenty of time to pray. Make good use of it!

OPTIONAL EXTRA

Make your prayer time at the end of the session feel a bit different by giving each group member a notecard, and having them write down a prayer for a specified member of the group, based on the themes and priorities of Jesus' prayer in John 17. Collect them and move on to a more general time of open prayer as normal. Later, mail each notecard to the appropriate group member. These will serve as a great encouragement, and a prompt to pray in return for other group members.

GUIDANCE FOR QUESTIONS

1. Describe your prayer life in three words. This discussion should hopefully throw up some interesting (and revealing) answers. For most of us, our prayer life is not what we'd like it to be!

2. What does Jesus mean when he says that "the hour has come" (v 1)? This "hour" is the hour or time of the cross. Jesus is saying that this is his supreme moment—a moment of glory (v 1). The place where God is most glorified is not in creation, not in a sunset, but at the blood-stained cross and the empty tomb.

3. Who is the focus of this first section of prayer? Why do you think that is? In this first part of the prayer (v 1-5) Jesus is praying for himself. But this is in no way self-centered. The burden of these verses is the glory of God and of the Son.

• **What specifically does Jesus pray for (v 5)?** For God to be glorified as the Son is glorified. Jesus' work has brought glory to God the Father (v 4) because he has completed what he was asked to do. In particular, the completed work of Christ on the cross glorifies God. The glory also belongs to Jesus: the glory of the cross is no less than the glory that Christ had with the Father before the world began (v 5).

4. What do these verses reveal about the workings of the Trinity? Verse 2 indicates one God in different Persons, who have different roles. God the Father granted authority to the Son; the Son gives eternal life to all those the Father has given him. If anyone tells you that to submit to authority is to demean your identity, point them to this verses. Jesus is no less than God, but in the mystery of the Trinity, he receives from and obeys the Father. The Father gives the Son the authority to give his people eternal life—eternal life is the gift of God. And, as with all gifts, all that is required is for us to receive. Conversely, we ourselves are God the Father's gift to Jesus.

5. Who is the focus of this second section of prayer [in 17:6-19]? In verses 6-19 Jesus prays for his disciples—the Twelve gathered around him and, by extension, his followers today. How encouraging it is that Jesus intercedes for us!

• **Why do you think that is? (What is Jesus aiming for in v 8, v 11a, v 13?)** Jesus prays for his disciples because they belong to him—they are the ones who "believed" (v 8). Soon Jesus will return to the Father and leave his disciples in the world—and so he prays for them in his absence (v 11a). Jesus' intention is that he might be glorified by his disciples, and that they might have the "full measure of … joy" that comes from knowing him (v 13). It is tempting to think sometimes that God's desire is merely for our begrudging

obedience. But Jesus' desire is for our joy—to be as joyful as it is humanly possible to be!

• **What specifically does he pray for (v 11, 15, 17)?** In verse 11 Jesus prays for his disciples' protection in a world that will be in opposition to them. In verse 15 Jesus asks that his disciples be protected from the evil one. The spiritual battle is real. The power of the evil one is great; Christ's power is greater. Given that we are surrounded by hate in this world, it would seem natural that Jesus would want us to leave the world, or to put as much distance between ourselves and the world around us as possible. But Jesus does not pray for those things. He prays that we would be protected as we live in this world, and seek to love those who are in love with this world. In verse 17 Jesus prays for his disciples to be sanctified—to become more like him, more holy. So while we are to remain *in* the world (v 15), there is no excuse for worldliness or sinfulness. We are not *of* the world (v 16).

⊗

• **How are we sanctified?** "By the truth; [God's] word is truth" (v 17). The person who wishes to be holy will be a person who reads the Bible, studies the Bible, learns the Bible, and trusts the Bible, and therefore has their mind and heart rewired by God's word. It's in this way that we increasingly put into practice the character of Christ, which God's word reveals. Behind sinful habits there is always a lie, and the tool for release is always "by the truth; your word is truth."

EXPLORE MORE
What is Jesus doing right now [Romans 8:33-34]? Jesus is interceding for us—he

is representing us before his Father and pleading our innocence on the basis of his death and resurrection on our behalf. **Where is he, and why is that significant?** He died, was raised to life, and is now at the right hand of God—he therefore has the Father's "ear", so to speak, so his prayers are effective. Jesus completed the work of "the hour" that he anticipated in John 17:1 and so is loved by the Father.

About what, in particular, should this give us confidence, according to these verses? Why? Nothing and no one can condemn us. This should be of great comfort when we feel the weight of our sin or feel worn down by our own weakness. God has chosen us, and Christ has saved us, so "no one" can condemn us.

6. APPLY: Look at verses 15-16. How do you think you're doing with being *in* the world but not *of* the world? In what ways do you struggle to get the balance right? This is the great balancing act of every Christian: to be "in" the world but not "of" the world. Present physically and inserted culturally, yet spiritually different, distinct, other, holy. All attempts at removal from the world altogether fail as a means of sanctifying us, for they do not deal with the ongoing presence of sin in our hearts. What we must seek is not to be removed out of the world physically but grow to be increasingly not of the world spiritually.

7. Who is the focus of this third section of prayer (v 20)? In verses 20-26 Jesus focuses on praying for all believers. Jesus begins by praying also "for those who will believe in me through their message"—in other words, all "not-yet Christians".

8. What specifically does he pray for,

and why?

- **v 21-23:** Jesus prays for unity among all believers—"complete unity" (v 23). He wants us to be "one"; and lest we downplay the extent of that unity, he asks specifically that we be one in the same way that he is in the Father and the Father is in him. This could not be a greater, or higher, definition of unity! Why? Jesus' aim is inherently missional. He wants the world to "believe that you have sent me" (v 21), and to "know that you sent me and have loved [Jesus' disciples]" (v 23). One of the greatest apologetics for the truth of the gospel is this organic unity of God's people.

- **v 24:** Jesus' prayer, and his purpose, is that we would see his glory and be with him in glory for all eternity. How quickly we forget our former slavery to sin, and how easy it is for us to doubt God's good purposes when we go through difficulties now. At times this life is a journey through continuous challenges. But at the end of the journey, there is glory!

- **v 26:** This is the grand purpose of Christ: to reveal the Father God to us. By his Spirit, he will continue to make God the Father known through his word. This is all for the purpose of love: "in order that the love you have for me may be in them and that I myself may be in them." What an extraordinary thought: the love that God has for the Son, through faith in Christ, we now have in us. And Christ himself is now in us, connected to us, invested in us. Who would want to be anything other than a disciple of Christ?!

⊻

- **Jesus is praying for unity, not uniformity. How does thinking about the nature of the Trinity help us to**

understand the difference? Father, Son and Spirit are completely united, and yet also distinct Persons. We should not, then, expect or desire a kind of unity that blurs distinctions. Jesus here is not praying for institutional uniformity or for the absence of denominational or cultural differences. What is more, Jesus' prayer has been answered. All true disciples of Jesus *are* one, as the Father is in the Son and the Son is in the Father. We know from experience that true Christians pray together, work together, support one another, and are fundamentally, organically, united.

EXPLORE MORE
Why do you think we are told to "keep" unity, not "create" unity (Ephesians 4:3)? What does that imply? Maintaining unity is hard work; you have to fight, spiritually-speaking, for unity. But Paul does not ask the Ephesians to create unity, because that unity has been created through Christ's unity with the Father, by means of our faith in Christ and the indwelling of the Spirit (in answer to Jesus' prayer in John 17:21). **What would it look like for you to "make every effort" to maintain unity within your church family? (Look at Ephesians 3:2 and v 4-6 for ideas)** We need to be patient with each other, overlooking little mistakes and differences of opinion, and being humble enough to accept that we won't always get our way. We need to speak gently, not harshly, so that we do not cause division (v 2). We should remember and thank God for the foundational beliefs we hold in common (v 4-6). More broadly, we are to celebrate the organic unity that we do enjoy. Praying together, doing evangelism together, holding conferences together, encouraging

one another, speaking well of each other, praising God for the unity in Christ that we do have—all this is necessary and good.

9. From what we've seen in John 17, describe Jesus' "prayer life" in three words. The idea is to draw together everything you've seen in this study, and to compare Jesus' prayer life with the words you chose to describe your own prayer life in question 1. There's no one right answer to this question, but words you might choose could include God-glorifying, spiritually-focused, sanctifying, unifying, loving.

10. APPLY: How could you make your prayer life more closely resemble Jesus' model here? In particular, think about...

• **who you pray for.** We should be praying for one another as disciples, especially within the context of our churches. Verse 20 implies that we should pray for those who are not yet Christians too. Take some time, if you have not already done so, to make a list of those known to you personally who are not yet Christians and pray for them regularly. Furthermore, one way we can share Christ's concern for unity is by praying for other local churches. We are not in competition with one another but are part of the same mission.

• **what you pray for.** We should be praying for God to be glorified (not merely for what is easy for us), for spiritual protection (not merely physical protection), for sanctification (not merely prosperity or for things to "go well"). We should be praying for increasing unity and love within our church community, so that others might believe in Christ through our message (v 20).

5 John 18:1-27
BETRAYAL AND DENIAL

THE BIG IDEA
When faced with opposition, Jesus faithfully submits to arrest, whereas Peter fearfully denies his Lord. Jesus' faithfulness offers hope when we fail him.

SUMMARY
This section of John's Gospel moves from teaching to narrative. Jesus leads his disciples to a garden where Judas meets them with an armed mob. The betrayal is complete. Yet Jesus' authority is unmistakable—the soldiers fall over at the sound of his voice (v 6). Jesus is not being forced; he is willingly carrying out the Father's plan and is taking care of his disciples as he does so (v 8-9). Armed resistance is not necessary (v 10-11).

The action moves to the high priest's home, where Jesus is brought for questioning, with Peter and another disciple following behind. John intentionally switches scenes between Peter (outside in the courtyard, v 15-18, 25-27) and Jesus (inside, v 19-24). Both face questions; but their responses could not be more different. Peter fails to stand up under questioning. Once so full of bravado, now he denies even being one of Jesus' disciples, just as Jesus predicted in 13:38. Yet Jesus walks faithfully toward his death, submitting himself to the indignity of unjust questions and physical violence. It is his faithfulness, and his willingness to die, that offers hope for repentant failures like Peter, and like us.

OPTIONAL EXTRA
The scenes we read in this study and the next are so multi-layered and filled with pathos that it is hard—perhaps impossible—to do it all justice. One of the best descriptions of these events comes in *The Lion, the Witch and the Wardrobe*. C. S. Lewis's descriptions of Aslan's walk to the garden with Susan and Lucy by his side are filled with all the right kinds of emotion: sadness, heaviness, horror—and then a final, thrilling joy. In order to set the tone at the start of the study, show your group the relevant clip from a movie or TV version of the book.

GUIDANCE FOR QUESTIONS
1. In what kinds of situations or relationships are you most tempted to speak or act as if you don't know Jesus? Allow your group to share examples—there may be particular family members or work situations where it is hard for people to speak and act in a way that is consistent with their faith. Come back to these examples when you get to apply questions 11 and 12.

2. Where does this scene take place? How does Judas know he will find Jesus there? Jesus and the disciples cross the Kidron Valley (symbolic in the Bible for various reasons: see 2 Samuel 15:23, Jeremiah 31:38-40, Zechariah 14:4), and walk through to a garden (which Matthew 26:36 tells us is Gethsemane). Judas knew this place well, because "Jesus had often met there with his disciples" (John 18:2), and so Jesus' choice of this location for his mini-retreat with his disciples was surely deliberate. He went where he knew that Judas could find him.

- **Why does this make his betrayal even more shocking?** The garden was a safe place where Jesus met with his inner circle. Judas used the knowledge gained in his position of an "insider" to turn his master over to his enemies.

3. Look at verse 4. If Jesus knows what is about to happen, why does he ask the crowd who they want? Jesus' question is not for his information—he knows the answer—but for the crowd's consideration. *Who is it that they want? Why have they really come?* Jesus is using a question to reveal what is in their hearts, so that they might—even at this hour, perhaps—turn and believe. But they neatly dodge the implications of Jesus' question by emphasizing Jesus' human nature, and (to them) disreputable origin. They have come just for "Jesus of Nazareth" (v 5, 7).

4. Twice the mob say they have come for "Jesus of Nazareth". What do Jesus' two responses tell us about him?

- **v 5-6:** Judas could pick Jesus out from the rest of the crowd without Jesus needing to tell him. But some extraordinary power is revealed as Jesus declares who he is: literally, Jesus says, "I am." Often (although not always) this "I am" construction in John seems to indicate the divine epithet "I AM"/ Yahweh (4:26; 6:20; and, most famously, 8:58). So as Jesus replies, "I am," and those who have come to arrest him "fell to the ground," what is being displayed is the power of the name of God, and the identity of Jesus as the great "I am."

- **v 8-9:** Jesus asks the crowd to let the disciples go. Even at his most extreme moment, being betrayed, Jesus is thinking about his disciples. He loves his disciples, including us—he has given his life that he might save us. We can trust him.

5. Why does Jesus tell Peter to put his sword away (v 10-11)? Jesus is going to fulfill the plan of God to sacrifice himself to save us, and Peter should not try to stop it (v 11b). The fact that Malchus is named shows us that this was a real person; but he was also a person for whom Jesus really cared. Such is our Lord: he loves his enemies. Peter needed to think before using a sword to protect the almighty King of love.

6. What details in verses 13-14 suggest that Jesus' trial will not be a fair one? The soldiers and officials bring Jesus to "Annas" (v 13), the father-in-law of Caiaphas, the high priest that year. The apparent nepotism of the senior leadership of the temple only underlines their corruption. Ironically, Caiaphas was the one who had advised the Jewish leaders that it would be good if one man died for the people (v 14). Jesus is about to appear before the court of a man who had already publicly declared that it would be best for everyone if Jesus was put to death (11:50). There is no semblance even of a fair trial.

EXPLORE MORE
In what sense was Caiaphas right? Jesus would die in the place of many people—and not only for the Jewish nation but for the whole world (people from every nation). And this is, in the truest sense of the word, "good" (18:14).
Why do you think John chooses to remind us of this detail in 18:14? How does it help us to understand what is going on? What does it teach us about the way God works?
John is reminding us that it is God who is in sovereign control of the unfolding events. Man may work his worst, and even kill the Son of God, but in so doing, he is only ever

fulfilling the purpose of God: to save all who believe through Jesus' own death and resurrection. It is useless to fight against God. Therefore, we are called to turn to him in repentance and faith.

7. APPLY: Jesus is powerful in the face of opposition and yet submits to his Father's will. He knows that his Father is sovereign over what he is about to suffer and will use evil to achieve good purposes. How should that mindset help you to have peace in the face of trouble? Jesus is powerful—18:6 shows us that he could have avoided arrest if he had wanted to! Yet he willingly walked toward the cross, because in the sovereignty of God it would indeed "be good if one man died for the people" (v 14). He is the "I AM", who is on our side. What is comforting in our suffering is not that God knows nothing about it, but that he knows *all* about it and has planned it for some good end that is as yet invisible to us (Romans 8:28). Evil men plotted to kill the Son of God, but in so doing fulfilled God's saving purposes. If we are being opposed by those who are fighting against God, we must remember that even that attack has a purpose.

8. What is striking about how events unfold in the courtyard (v 15-18, 25-27)? There is no one right answer to this question—the aim is simply to get your group looking at and thinking about the details of this colorful narrative. Your group might notice, for instance, that it is a mere servant girl that Peter is afraid of in verse 17! There is a hint of a sneer in the question that reminds us of the temptations of Genesis 3: "Did God really say…? You will not certainly die" (Genesis 3:1, 4). John 18:18 is classic John: "It was cold." He is using the description of the elements to accent the mood and atmosphere, spiritually as well as emotionally. Or how about the intriguing details in verse 26? A relative of the person whose ear Peter had cut off notices him—surely if anyone would recognize Peter it was this man!

Some members of your group might want to know who the "other disciple" was (v 15-16). Many have said that the "other disciple" must be John, the "beloved disciple" (which it almost certainly is in 20:2-4, 8). Others think it is unlikely that a fisherman was so closely connected to the high priest, meaning this "other disciple" must be someone else (18:15 suggests that he was possibly a kinsman). The truth is that we do not know for sure who this "other disciple" was! Why then does John mention him? Perhaps he intended to contrast Peter's denial with this anonymous disciple's faithfulness at this point. Peter may have had a reputation among the disciples and within the early church, but that does not guarantee you faithfulness in adversity.

• **How well does Peter stand up under questioning?** He fails miserably and repeatedly. Be sure to draw your group's attention back to 13:37-38. When under questioning, Peter should have done what he had predicted he would do and publicly affirmed his allegiance to Christ even at risk of his own life.

9. How well does Jesus stand up under questioning in verses 19-24? He keeps his cool and responds with reason. He doesn't perjure himself or lie to save his own neck. He knows where this trial is heading, and he is prepared to go there.

• **Put his replies in your own words.** Jesus' reply in 18:20-21 is brilliant. Basically, he is saying that if the high priest really wants to know what Jesus has been teaching, all he has to do is ask the people who have heard Jesus. He has not taught anything in secret. This protects Jesus from having to recount every little detail of what he has said for cross-examination. It also makes it clear that the high priest is not really looking for information; he is trying to spring a trap. Likewise, in verse 23, Jesus' logic exposes his accuser's injustice and sin: *If I've done something wrong, prove it. But if I haven't, why are you hitting me?*

10. Why does John put verses 19-24 between the two scenes in the courtyard, do you think? Draw your group's attention to the word "meanwhile" in verses 19 and 25. The scene changes in verse 19 to heighten the tension of what is about to happen—we're left on a momentary cliffhanger and have to wait to find out if the second and third denials will come just as Jesus predicted. In verse 25 the scene switches back again to Peter, who is held up as a direct contrast to Christ. He is not standing as Christ did.

11. APPLY: "Peter was just as bad as Judas." Do you agree? Why/why not? Give your group some time to discuss varying opinions. Ultimately, though, Judas and Peter are not the same and are not just as bad as each other. Be careful to distinguish between denying as Peter did and betraying as Judas did. Peter's story ends in repentance and restoration; Judas' story ends in judgment (see Matthew 27:1-10).

• **Satan would love to convince us that our denials make us a Judas, not a Peter. How does the ending to Peter's story (see John 21:15-19) help us when we feel guilty for letting Jesus down?** We must not allow Satan to convince us that our denials make us a Judas (nor

the opposite—that they're justifiable). Peter will be wooed back to faith and commitment and discipleship by Jesus himself (21:15). We too can follow Christ again even after we have denied him. If Peter could be so greatly used by God after he three times denied Christ, then so can we. After all, now, in Christ, there is no condemnation (Romans 8:1). Use this question to make sure this study ends on a note of grace, not guilt.

12. APPLY: How does Christ's faithfulness help us to stay faithful under pressure? Encourage your group to reflect on the note in the study guide and share what has thrilled them about Jesus from this passage. It's as we look to Christ and his love for us that we will grow in love for him and walk closely with him. This, in turn, will help us to risk our relationships, our reputations, and even more, for his sake.

6 John 18:28 – 19:42
THE GLORY OF THE CROSS

THE BIG IDEA
Jesus is the true King, the one with real authority—yet he died on the cross as our substitute, in order to deal with our sin once and for all.

SUMMARY
We've arrived at the climax of John's Gospel. John's passion narrative describes what is happening, while also pointing to what it really means. What looks like a scene of defeat, weakness, and shame is in fact where Christ's glory is most clearly displayed, as he offers himself as the true Passover Lamb to die in the place of his people.

The courtroom drama of 18:28 – 19:16 is thick with irony. Pilate's posturing makes him look like the one in authority, yet it is the Jews who force his hand toward execution. Pilate himself comes to the conclusion that Jesus is innocent, and becomes increasingly fearful as the scene unfolds. Jesus shows no such fear or weakness at the prospect of his crucifixion; he is a King, although not yet of this world (18:36), and Pilate's authority is only that which has been given to him from God (19:11). And so, just as Jesus predicted, he is handed over to be crucified (18:16).

John's crucifixion account is rich with Old Testament allusions which point to its meaning (two of which are explored in the Explore More sections). John is keen, first, that we understand that Jesus' death was all according to God's plan; and second, that we understand that Jesus really died—his side was pierced, releasing a flow of blood and water, and he was buried in a tomb.

This study focuses on Jesus' declaration in 19:30: "It is finished." God's salvation plan for sin is complete. No work of ours can add to our salvation; no sin of ours can detract from it. All we must do is respond in faith: the eyewitness testimony of the cross is given "so that you also may believe" (v 35).

OPTIONAL EXTRA
Split your group into teams, and have each team list what they think are the ten strongest animals in the world (in proportion to their body weight). According to one website, those are grizzly bear, anaconda, elephant, musk ox, tiger, eagle, gorilla, leafcutter ant, rhinoceros beetle and, strongest of all, the dung beetle (which can pull 1141 times its body weight). How many did each team guess correctly? Were there any surprises as you read out the answers? The point is that, when it comes to power and weakness, looks can often be deceiving (see question 1).

GUIDANCE FOR QUESTIONS
1. "Looks can be deceiving." How have you seen this play out when it comes to the areas of weakness and strength? This is an opportunity for your group to discuss occasions when people have looked weak but turned out to be strong or powerful, and vice versa. You might like to think about physical strength, influence in the workplace or social groups, political power, etc.

2. When are these events happening (18:28)? At Passover time, the festival that commemorated the rescue of the Israelites from slavery in Egypt. **Why is that significant?** At the first Passover, the Israelites were saved from God's judgment by substitution—a lamb was killed in the place of the firstborn son in each family (see Exodus 12). John is hinting at the fact that Jesus is the true Passover Lamb, who, although completely innocent, will die in the place of his people (we'll see this idea again in John 19:36). In 18:28 John also notes an astonishing irony: the Jews will not enter the Roman palace for fear of ceremonial uncleanness! These are men who have just aided and abetted a serious miscarriage of justice, and are now attempting to convince the pagan Roman governor to do their dirty work for them—and they are worried about "ceremonial uncleanness"?!

3. For each party, note in the left-hand column the verse references or details that suggest they are in a position of power. Then note in the right-hand column the verse references or details that suggest they are in a position of weakness. If you have a big group, you could split them into three smaller groups to investigate one "character" each before reporting back to the group as a whole. See table below for things to look out for. The point of this exercise is to show that while Pilate looks to be in a position of power, it is the Jewish leaders who hold all the influence… and yet events are unfolding according to God's sovereign plan. Despite looking weak in the world's eyes, Jesus is the true King—he is putting himself in a position of weakness in order to win salvation for those who acknowledge him as King.

	POWER	WEAKNESS
JEWISH LEADERS	18:28 – the Jewish leaders are physically in charge of Jesus and bring him to Pilate. 18:40 – they demand Barabbas' release, despite Pilate's reluctance. 19:4-7 – Jesus being flogged isn't enough to satisfy them—they push for the death sentence. 19:12 – they threaten Pilate.	18:31 – they have no right to execute anyone under Roman law—only Pilate can do that.
PILATE	18:33-37 – Pilate is questioning Jesus, appearing to stand in judgment over him. 19:1 – At Pilate's command, Jesus is flogged and mocked. 19:10 – Pilate has the legal power to set Jesus free or execute him. 19:13-14 – Pilate sits in the judge's seat—he has judicial authority.	18:38-40 – Pilate tries to have Jesus released for the Passover, but the religious leaders resist. 19:5-6 – Pilate hopes the flogging will be enough to satisfy the Jewish leaders, but it is not. 19:8-9 – Pilate is afraid. He can tell Jesus is no ordinary criminal, but he is backed into a corner by the religious leaders. 19:12 – Pilate tries to set Jesus free, but he is unable to.

POWER	WEAKNESS
JESUS 18:32 – Jesus knew that all this was going to happen; events are unfolding to fulfill his word (e.g. 8:28, 12:24, 12:32). 18:36 – Jesus is King—his kingdom is not a political one but a spiritual one. 18:37 – Jesus has come to bring truth—the truth of the gospel and our need for it. Those who do not listen to him will not be saved. 19:7-8 – Pilate is afraid of Jesus. 19:9-11 – Pilate's authority is ultimately from God.	18:28 – Jesus is physically taken from one "trial" to another. 19:1-3 – Jesus is beaten and mocked—he looks like no king at all. 19:16 – Jesus is handed over to be crucified.

4. So, who killed Jesus? The answer in the biblical account is deliberately nuanced. Pilate, a representative of Gentiles, passed sentence. The Jewish religious leaders, representatives of the Jewish people, urged that Jesus be killed. Both Jew and Gentile are implicated—and so, by extension, every human is implicated. But there is a further and in fact more profound nuance. According to John, all this was planned by Jesus himself (18:32). In the most important sense, then, we should say that "Jesus killed Jesus." As Joseph put it when he confronted and forgave the brothers who had sold him into slavery in Genesis 50:20: "You intended to harm me, but God intended it for good to accomplish what is now being done, the saving of many lives." Our sins—those of Jew and Gentile—nailed Jesus to the cross, and God's hand kept him there, and Jesus willingly went there.

EXPLORE MORE
What elements of Isaiah's prophecy [53:1-9] do you see being fulfilled in John 18:28 – 19:16? Jesus was despised and rejected by the Jewish leaders and the soldiers (Isaiah 53:3). He was silent when

questioned by Pilate (Isaiah 53:7). The verdict against him was unanimous, damning, and unjust (Isaiah 53:8). Pilate recognized his innocence—he "had done no violence" (Isaiah 53:9).
What does Isaiah's prophecy tell us about why all this happened? Encourage your group to linger on verses 5 and 6—he was crushed for our iniquities, so that we might have peace with God. This is beautiful truth indeed!

5. APPLY: What does this passage show you about your sin, and about your own need for a Saviour? We are wrong if we think that we would have behaved any differently if we were in the courtroom. This rejection of God's authority as King has been at the heart of sin since Genesis 3. John 19 is a mirror that reflects the shocking truth of our own ugly hearts—we are like this too, in our depravity. As much as we look at the cross and see our salvation, so we should also look at it and see how much we need the Savior. In those voices crying, "Crucify," we can hear our own accents too.

6. What do the following verses show

us about Jesus, and the purpose of his death?

- **v 19-22:** Unbeknown to Pilate and the chief priests, the sign speaks truth: this is "the king of the Jews," as well as the King of the universe. Notice the irony. The pagan Roman governor writes accurately; the Jewish leaders try to remove what has been said; and yet God in his sovereignty causes the sign to stay, as it is to witness to the truth of him who hangs beneath it.

- **v 23-24:** God's word is being fulfilled in the details of the cross. Although the soldiers are free agents, John wants to show us that what they are doing is nevertheless a consequence of what has been predicted: the "so" toward the end of verse 24 reminds us of this.

- **v 25-27:** In the moment of his own most dire need, Jesus ensures the needs of others are taken care of. He looks down from the cross and establishes a home for the mother losing her son. This is an outward hint of what cannot yet be seen—that at the moment of his greatest pain, Jesus is working out the greatest redemption. It is through his death that Jesus loves, looks after, and restores his followers.

- **v 28-30:** Again, Jesus shows his sovereignty as he ensures "that Scripture [is] fulfilled" (v 28). If Christ is in charge of this event, then we can be assured that he is in charge of all events; if Christ rules at the cross, then he rules at all times; if this cross completes the work of salvation, then, through faith in him, our sins are paid for: "It is finished".

EXPLORE MORE

In what way does [Psalm 22] point forward to the crucifixion account in John's Gospel? The original psalm was written of sufferings not directly related to crucifixion, and is accredited to King David during one or other of his troubles. Yet Psalm 22 now speaks of what is happening to and around Jesus and finds its ultimate fulfilment there. Psalm 22:18 is directly quoted in John 19:24, and Jesus' declaration that "it is finished" appears to echo Psalm 22:31: "He has done it!"

Why does it matter that the death of Jesus was no accident but a planned and prophesied event? This teaches us not to underestimate the power of God's word. The word of God is living and active, and its promises can be relied upon to be fulfilled in his time and according to his will. On the one hand, "it is finished" sounds like final defeat—Jesus has been overpowered by his enemies. But with the background of Psalm 22 in mind, and with the resurrection that we know is to come, the phrase "it is finished" sounds, rather, a note of triumph—the plan has been completed.

7. How does John show us that Jesus was really dead (v 31-37, 38-42)? First, John tells us that a soldier jabbed a spear up into Jesus' side (presumably to confirm that Jesus was really dead) and to his surprise, out came a "sudden flow of blood and water" (v 34). Modern doctors have confirmed that such a flow of "blood and water" would be a certain sign that the patient was definitively dead. It is often assumed that ancient peoples were as ignorant of death as the average modern person in the West, where death is kept at a distance. In the ancient world it was not so—these soldiers knew what they were doing. Second, John describes the burial of Jesus (v 38-42). There is more that can be said about these verses, but for the purposes of this study, the important fact to establish is that Jesus really was dead and buried.

- **Why is that important, do you think?**
This is important because the miracle of the resurrection of Jesus from the dead is only a miracle if Jesus were truly dead in the first place. We are meant to learn that Jesus definitely died, and so the resurrection was a true resurrection, from the dead.

8. What is the significance of the Scripture that John quotes in verses 36-37? John records the sudden flow of blood and water so that we might know that "the scripture [had been] fulfilled" (v 36). The first quotation—"Not one of his bones will be broken"—is either referring to the Passover lamb, whose bones were not to be broken (Exodus 12:46; Numbers 9:12), or to a prophetic interpretation of Psalm 34:20. The second quotation—"They will look on the one they have pierced"—is from Zechariah 12:10, where God promises to pour out a spirit of grace and mercy, while the people shall look on him whom they have pierced and mourn for him. The point John is making is that the death of Jesus is no accident but a planned and prophesied event. It is connected to the Passover Lamb of God, given to us as a fulfillment of all that the Exodus lamb pictured, to finally and completely take away the sins of God's people.

9. APPLY: In what ways do we sometimes think or act as though it is not finished?
- **What will it look like to live out the words "It is finished" this week?**
We must never add anything to the completed work of Christ on the cross. It is easy to start with grace but then continue with works; the devil loves to turn a Christian into a legalist when he can, and bind him with chains of unnecessary guilt or pride or habitual sin. We need to remember: *it is finished*. No work of ours can add to our salvation; no sin of ours can detract from it. There is nothing more to be done than has already been done at the cross! A Christian is never much good for anything until he or she is sure that their eternal destiny is sealed in the finished work of Christ. That taken care of, we can focus on serving Christ out of an overflow of passion for him, no longer anxiously digging up the roots of our behavior to see if it is sufficient.

10. APPLY: How has reading this passage about your crucified King challenged your expectations of what following him will look like? The pattern we see in Christ (and the pattern for the Christian life) is one of glory through suffering. We suffer now, and the vindication of resurrection comes later. Until that day, we should not expect the Christian life to be easy. Yet there is joy too—we are forgiven! So now we too strive for "the same mindset as Christ Jesus" (Philippians 2:5), not scorning shame and not shirking obedience, but putting to death our selfish self so that we might rise with Christ to new life. His death has paid the price for our sin; and in his death we too must put to death the deeds of the flesh by the power of the risen Christ in us, so that we might die to sin and live for righteousness (Romans 6:11-14).

7 John 20:1-31
LIFE IN HIS NAME

THE BIG IDEA

The resurrection was a real, historical event that shows us that Jesus is the Messiah and the Son of God. He calls us to hear and believe, so that we might enjoy resurrection life ourselves and share it with others.

SUMMARY

We start the study at the end of the passage, with John's "purpose statement" (20:30-31). John's reason for writing his Gospel, and recording the resurrection as he does, is that we might believe that Jesus is who he says he is and therefore have life in his name. As you proceed through the study, it is worth coming back to this question at various points: "How does this detail help us to believe that Jesus is the Messiah and the Son of God?"

The first witness to the empty tomb is Mary Magdalene, closely followed by Peter and "the other disciple", John (v 1-10). The assumption is that someone has taken the body (v 2), not that Jesus has been raised. But John's careful description of the neatly folded grave clothes casts this theory into doubt, and it is enough to convince John himself that Jesus is alive ("he saw and believed", v 8).

Mary is still distraught at the idea that her Lord's body has been shamefully stolen. Jesus lovingly reveals himself to her but tells her not to hold on to him. Instead he sends her to tell his disciples the news. When Jesus appears to the gathered disciples that evening, he speaks of sending them with a message of peace and forgiveness, in the power of the Holy Spirit. The implication is

clear: the resurrection is news to be shared.

In verses 24-29 we read the famous account of "doubting Thomas." Jesus is gracious (he offers Thomas the proof that he needs) but also calls him to "stop doubting and believe" (v 27). Jesus' words in verse 29 come with a twist: Thomas and the other disciples have believed because they have seen (v 8, 27), but Jesus says that it is more blessed to believe *without* seeing. Generations to come will believe on the basis of *hearing* the apostles' testimony, including John's Gospel. How wonderful it is to know that our risen Messiah calls us blessed!

OPTIONAL EXTRA

Print out a range of news headlines: some of them real and some of them fake (you can find examples of "fake news" online, or have fun writing your own). See if your group can distinguish the fact from the fiction. Afterwards, discuss how they came to their decisions. How do we know what to believe and what not to believe? (e.g. likelihood of the claim, how reputable the source is, whether there are holes in the story.) Although the resurrection sounds unlikely, the eyewitness testimony stacks up.

GUIDANCE TO QUESTIONS

1. Have you ever received some news that seemed too good to be true? What was it, and how did you respond?
Encourage your group to share a variety of examples, and be ready with your own. The initial confusion and disbelief at the empty tomb shows that Jesus' resurrection at first seemed "too good to be true" for the

disciples. We will come back to this idea in questions 4 and 9.

2. What does John say is the reason why he has written what he has written?

Note how selective John is in the use of his material. There are many other signs that Jesus did (21:25), but they are not included here. So why choose these particular signs? John's purpose is to bring us to faith—true belief in and commitment to Christ. In particular, we are to believe that this Jesus is the Messiah (or Christ, which means the same), and the Son of God, so that we might have life in his name.

• **What does it mean to have "life in his name"?** "Life" in John is not merely the absence of death or the presence of existence. John 1:4 says: "In [the Word] was life, and that life was the light of all mankind." This is the life that is on offer! And this is what Jesus has come to give us: "I have come that they may have life, and have it to the full" (10:10). In Christ, we are brought back into communion with Life itself, such that we live forever by entering into the experience of that life now. John wrote to point us to it and to invite us to enjoy it.

3. What do the following people find when they go to the tomb, and what conclusions do they come to?

• **Mary:** Tombs were cut into the rock and had large stones rolled over the entrance to prevent animals and grave robbers from disturbing the graves. But this stone has been removed from the entrance: no small feat. Mary's emotional response to the empty tomb is evident in 20:2: "She came running." Her response is understandable,

but still not one of understanding: "They have taken the Lord out of the tomb, and we don't know where they have put him!" *What extra scandal is this? Can they not even let him be now that he is dead?* Mary is still in the dark as to why the tomb is empty.

• **Peter:** Peter arrives after John and goes straight into the tomb—he "saw the strips of linen lying there" (v 6-7). What strikes them both at this stage is that the body has gone, *but the grave clothes remain*. If this were a grave robber, what would be the point of taking the body and leaving the linen clothes? Moreover, Peter notices that the burial cloth that has been around Jesus' head is "still lying in its place, separate from the linen." How tidy was this grave robber! Why is the burial cloth for the head separate from the rest—unless it was removed and placed down in a different location as each part was taken off?

• **John ("the other disciple"):** When John went into the tomb, he "saw and believed" (v 8). What did he believe? In the context of John (especially 20:30-31), it can only mean that he believed that Jesus was who he said was, the Son of God, and that now—in seeing this empty tomb and the graveclothes—he believed that Jesus had risen from the dead. The disciples did not come to the empty tomb expecting Jesus to have risen from the dead (v 9). They were not acting out of "wish-fulfilment". John was persuaded purely on the basis of what his eyes saw.

4. "If it seems too good to be true, it usually is." How does Mary show something of that attitude in these verses? Mary is mourning; the one she has so loved is dead, and she has no idea

what is now going on (v 11-12). Where is the body? Mary's anguished answer to the angels in verse 13 shows that while John may have "believed" already (v 8), Mary clearly had not. Having given her answer to the question of the angels, she turns around and sees Jesus—but she does not realize that it is Jesus (v 14), perhaps precisely because it seems too good to be true. Mary thinks he is the gardener, and leaps to the conclusion that perhaps he knows where the body might be.

5. Verse 16 is a beautiful moment. But why does Jesus tell Mary not to hold on to him (v 17)? "For I have not yet returned to my Father." This seems a strange reason to give for a strange objection. The point is that Mary, while appropriately adoring Jesus, now has a task to do. The attitude that Jesus encourages is not one of passive amazement but one of active mission. They are not to cling onto him, but to share him. To paraphrase the angelic message at the ascension, *Why are you just standing there? Get out on mission!* (Acts 1:11).

- **What task does he give her?** "Go instead to my brothers and tell them." Her task is to witness to the one she has seen—not just the empty tomb but the risen Jesus himself. She must also speak of the resurrection's significance: "I am ascending to my Father and your Father, to my God and your God" (John 20:17). In other words, the work of Jesus on the cross has opened up the throneroom of heaven, so that Jesus' disciples can have an intimate relationship with the Father through faith in the Son. God is their Father as well as the Son's Father!

6. What words might you have expected the risen Jesus to first say to his disciples? Let your group have some

fun imagining various alternatives. Perhaps: "Why are you hiding in this room with the doors locked? Did you not know that I was going to rise again? How many times did I tell you! And you're still afraid! Ridiculous."

- **Why is it significant that the first thing he says is "Peace be with you!"?** It is wonderful that Jesus' first words are words of peace. Jesus came to give us true peace—wholeness, completeness, a sense of being as we were made to be. His death and resurrection secure this for us. Like the disciples, we ought to be overjoyed (v 20)!

7. What task does he give them? Jesus gives them a mission: "As the Father has sent me, I am sending you" (v 21). The presence of Jesus gives peace and joy, and the commission of Jesus commands us to share that peace and joy by sharing him. But this is not a task that is done in our own strength or power. It requires and relies upon the filling of the Holy Spirit (v 22). It is he who convicts of sin; it is he who opens hearts to receive the gospel; it is he who gives gifts to extend the gospel to all nations.

Note: How is it that the Holy Spirit could be given here and also on the day of Pentecost (Acts 2:1-4)? There are several ways to read this, but the one I tend toward is that the Holy Spirit was given here as he was in the Old Testament—for times of special anointing and power (e.g. Exodus 31:3; Deuteronomy 34:9; Judges 3:10; 6:34). The gift of the Spirit at Pentecost was new in that the Spirit was given to all believers, to take the gospel to all nations and languages (Acts 2:6). This giving of the Spirit in John 20 is a precursor and preparation for the giving of the Spirit at Pentecost.

8. APPLY: How has what you have read in this passage…

- **reminded you of what the gospel message is?** The gospel message is an offer of peace, forgiveness, and eternal life through faith in Jesus, the Messiah and the Son of God. He is the King who died in our place, and his resurrection is God's seal of approval on all his claims and promises. Although we are not eyewitnesses to the resurrection, through God's word we have experienced the resurrection power of Jesus, and it is our task to tell others about what Jesus has done for us: "I have seen the Lord!" (v 18).

- **excited you about what the gospel message is?** Give your group time and space to reflect on what good news this is.

9. APPLY: Jesus' disciples were not expecting Jesus to come back to life. All of them had to be persuaded of it. How might this be helpful as we seek to engage with sceptical friends? The disciples were not stupid or gullible—and Christians aren't required to be stupid or gullible either! But the Christian faith is nothing if Christ has not risen bodily from the dead. And the truth of this resurrection is based not upon the experimental dictates of science, nor is it based only on arguments of logic; but it is based upon history, upon eyewitness accounts. The resurrection of Jesus is presented by John as something that happened, and for all our desire to present the resurrection as meaningful in an emotional sense, that meaning is only sustainable if it is rooted where John roots the story: in historical fact. It's worth engaging with sceptics on this point: what other explanations are there for the empty tomb? Do they add up? When all things are considered, the resurrection of Jesus starts to be seen as the most credible option.

EXPLORE MORE
What do [Romans 8:29; 1 Corinthians 15:20-23; Colossians 1:18] tell us about the meaning of the resurrection? Christ is "firstborn among many brothers and sisters" (Romans 8:29); his resurrection is the "firstfruits," meaning that when he returns, "those who belong to him" will also be raised from the dead (1 Corinthians 15:23). What is more, the resurrection also declares Christ's supremacy over the church and over all things: "He is the beginning and the firstborn from among the dead, so that in everything he might have the supremacy" (Colossians 1:18). All this majestic level of meaning is present at the empty tomb in John 20.

How does this excite you, and give you confidence, about what will happen to you when you die? Christ's resurrection is what guarantees our resurrection. We are heading for eternity in a real, resurrection body—something like our own now but super-charged with strength and glory. This really is something to look forward to!

10. In what way is Jesus gracious to Thomas? Thomas is usually known as "Doubting Thomas," though this is a little unfair, because Thomas was really only asking for the same evidence that the other disciples had had (20:24). A week later, Jesus appears and invites Thomas to do exactly what it is that Thomas has insisted he will need to do if he is to believe (v 25, 27). Thomas wants evidence; and Jesus does give him the evidence that he demands.

- **In what way does Jesus challenge Thomas?** Jesus gives Thomas a rebuke: "Stop doubting and believe." It is a rebuke that some of us, as natural skeptics, need to hear on occasion. The old illustration of a chair is still effective. You may think that a chair can hold your weight, but real belief involves sitting down on it! Thomas is here being told to trust Jesus: to actually believe.

11. APPLY: John saw and believed (v 8). Thomas saw and believed (v 29). What surprising thing does Jesus say in verse 29? Jesus notes that it is because Thomas has seen that he has believed, and then he "breaks the fourth wall" to address people like us, the readers of John's Gospel, who will believe not by seeing but by *hearing*: "Blessed are those who have not seen and yet have believed."

• **It is a more "blessed" situation to be reading the Bible than sitting outside the empty tomb on that first Easter Sunday or in the upper room a week later! How does that encourage you?** While the eyewitness experience of seeing the empty tomb must have been amazing, it should never be forgotten that the disciples' initial conclusion was despair or at least confusion. We, on the other hand, have the word of God preached to us, through the New Testament and the work of the Spirit through that word. Belief is a precious thing—if we have it, we are indeed blessed! This encourages us to keep on believing.

12. APPLY: How has what you have read in John 20 helped you "believe that Jesus is the Messiah, the Son of God"? This is an opportunity for your group to share the things that have struck them from this passage. What reassurances have they had about the reality of the resurrection? Where have they seen Jesus' power and grace?

• **What would it look like for you to truly enjoy having "life in his name" this week?** Jesus said, "I have come that they may have life, and have it to the full" (10:10). We can have peace, knowing that we are right with God; we can have confidence for the future, knowing that King Jesus is on the throne; we can have hope in the face of death, because his resurrection secures our own.

8 John 21:1-25
BREAKFAST BY THE SEA

THE BIG IDEA
Jesus feeds his disciples and then sends them out to feed others. His restoration of Peter shows us there is hope and forgiveness when we fail, and challenges us to extend that same hope and forgiveness to others.

SUMMARY
We come now toward the close of John's extraordinary narrative of the gospel of Jesus Christ, and to what is perhaps the best breakfast meeting ever. The appearances of Jesus to his disciples after his resurrection were not random but for particular purposes. This third appearance is for fellowship (21:1-14) and restoration for Peter (v 15-25).

The disciples are back on home territory, in Galilee, and they embark on an unsuccessful fishing trip—until, that is, Jesus appears and turns their empty catch into a "large number of fish" (v 6). John is the first to recognize Jesus (v 7, "It is the Lord!"), but Peter is the first to take action, swimming to the shore to meet Jesus, with the other disciples coming in behind on the boat. Jesus invites the disciples to "come and have breakfast," and they are stunned into silence. They know now for sure that it is Jesus. There comes a moment in the presence of the King when we find that our lips are closed as we simply wonder at who he is and delight in his love and provision for us.

Verses 15-21 bring us the reinstatement of Peter after his failure, and it is significant that it is this (and not any other possible ending) that John chooses to use as he brings his Gospel to a close. Clearly "life

... to the full" (10:10) really is on offer for those who believe (20:31)—including those who are flawed and who fail. Three times Jesus asks Peter, "Do you love me?" He wants to replace Peter's three-fold denial with a thrice-repeated protestation of love for Jesus, and a thrice-repeated commission to feed and care for Christ's sheep. But for Peter this will also be costly: in verse 18, Jesus predicts the kind of death that Peter will die for the sake of his Lord.

The application questions in this study focus on the invitation to enjoy personal fellowship with the Lord Jesus, the importance of feeding and caring for Christ's people with the word of God, and the promise of restoration when, like Peter, we fail.

OPTIONAL EXTRA
The senses of taste and smell have a powerful way of stimulating our imagination. Cook some fish and bread for your group to eat as they arrive, to create something of the atmosphere of Jesus' breakfast on the beach.

GUIDANCE FOR QUESTIONS
1. "The church is the only army that shoots its wounded." Do you agree? Why / why not? This quote is deliberately provocative. The idea is that, for all our protestations of mercy and kindness, once someone fails within the "army" of the church, that mercy can sadly be in very short supply. Your group will have different ideas, depending on their own experiences. Be careful to ensure this discussion does not descend into gossip or finger-pointing.

2. Describe the scene in verse 3. What do you think the disciples are thinking or feeling? The disciples are back on home territory, in Galilee, and are doing what they were trained to do—fishing—while they await further instructions. But on this night they have not caught anything. We can imagine they might have felt tired, disappointed, and hungry!

3. What do verses 4-6 tell us about Jesus? (See also v 12.) These verses dramatically, almost playfully, reveal God the Son's power. Jesus reveals (again) who he is by miraculously bringing into their net an extraordinarily large catch. That does not mean that the disciples do not need to work for it; they still have to let their nets down. But it is all at Jesus' command—he is indeed "the Lord" (v 7, 12).

- **What do verses 7-9 tell us about Peter?** Peter is the first to take action—he's often the disciple to take the initiative. He puts back on his outer garment (fishing naked, or at least scantily clad, would not have been uncommon). And he dives into the water to get to Jesus as quickly as he can. It's clear that he wants to see Jesus, and that he has respect for the Lord.

4. "Come and have breakfast," says Jesus in verse 12. Why is it significant that this is what Jesus chooses to do with his friends when he appears to them (v 1, 14)? Each appearance of the risen Jesus is intended to communicate that Jesus is indeed raised from the dead, and then to tell us something specific about his resurrection. The first appearance was to give the disciples peace, joy, and the Holy Spirit (20:19-23). The second was to give Thomas faith (20:24-29). This third appearance is for fellowship (and restoration for Peter). The Master is always relational

with his disciples. Church is to be a place of relationship, love and fellowship—with Christ and with each other. Draw your group's attention to verse 13: this was Jesus' characteristic way of eating with his disciples. He takes "the teapot" and (as the English say) "plays mother," giving out the food to the "kids" around him. He is the one who provides for and cares for his friends.

- **What words would you use to describe the atmosphere at this breakfast?** There is no one right answer to this question. Appropriate words would include: wonder, peace, joy and community.

5. APPLY: What would it look like for you to "come and have breakfast" with Jesus? We must be those who will take the time—with the Bible open and our hearts open to God through prayer by the Holy Spirit—to be with Jesus: to sit with him and learn from him. In the busyness of our "fishing"—home-making, work, ministry—we need to ensure that we have time to "have breakfast" with Jesus. This doesn't necessarily have to be first thing in the morning, of course, although many find that a helpful way to start the day.

6. APPLY: Look at your answers to the second part of question 4. Have you experienced something similar in your fellowship with Jesus? Share specific examples. The aim of this question is for your group to encourage one another with stories of times when they have experienced sweet communion with the Lord Jesus (and therefore spur one another on to seek the same). Be ready with your own example if your group are struggling.

7. Jesus now addresses an "elephant in

the room." **What is it?** Peter's denial of Jesus during his trial (see 18:15-18, 25-27). Remind your group of quite how shocking this was—Peter said three times that he didn't even know Jesus! This "elephant in the room" is not the first topic that Jesus broaches with Peter after the resurrection. But at the right time, sitting down together around a fire after an amazing catch of fish, Jesus starts to bring healing to Peter.

- **Why does Jesus ask Peter if he loves him more than the other disciples do (v 15, see 13:37)?** Peter, having placed himself ahead of the other disciples by claiming that he would lay down his life for Jesus (13:37), is now being asked whether his love really is greater than that of these other disciples. The bitter experience of failure has taught Peter to be humbler now than he once was—he does not reply that he loves Jesus more than the other disciples do, but merely that he loves Jesus (21:15).

- **Why does Jesus ask Peter three times whether he loves him (v 17, see 18:15-18, 25-27)?** The repetition causes Peter some hurt, surely because Jesus is seeking to raise in Peter's mind the memory of his thrice-repeated denial (21:17). It was good for Peter to hear himself say three times over, "I love you," when previously he had said three times over, "I don't know him." Sometimes we need to hear ourselves say something, in order to believe that we mean it. As the Master Shepherd, Jesus draws out of Peter the work of God in him, so that Peter might hear the love that he truly does have for Christ.

8. What does Jesus tell Peter to do (v 15, 16, 17)? What does he mean by this? Peter must "feed" the sheep and "take care" of the sheep. Feeding the flock with

God's word is at the heart of the pastoral office (see Explore More). But not only are pastors to preach; they are also to take care of the sheep in what we would call "pastoral care" and "pastoral counseling."

- **What will it involve for Peter (v 18)?** In this verse Jesus predicts the kind of death that Peter will die (as John's narrative aside in verse 19 makes clear). In being told that he will "stretch out [his] hands," Peter is being told that he will die on a cross. He is being called to be a shepherd, and shepherds must be ready to die to self for the sake of the flock (see 10:11). This is love in action.

EXPLORE MORE
Read 2 Timothy 4:1-5. What does feeding the sheep involve? Preaching the word, correcting, rebuking and encouraging—with care and patience (v 2). **What might it cost?** The fact that patience is required (v 2) and hardship is to be expected (v 5) shows that this task will not be easy. Some people will not want to hear the truth and will turn away or make life difficult for the pastor (v 3-4). **What is the warning here for church members? How should this passage, and John 21:15-23, shape our expectations of our church leaders?** We must be careful that we are not those with "itching ears," who are only prepared to listen to what we want to hear. We should expect to be lovingly rebuked and challenged by our leaders. Flocks need to be content with—and give thanks for—pastors who feed them with the word of God.

9. What do you think is behind Peter's question in verse 21? What do you make of Jesus' reply? If Peter is going to die a hard death, he wants to know whether John will die in the same way too!

Jesus' reply is, in essence, that it is none of Peter's business (v 22). Our responsibility is to love Jesus and to follow him. If we are called to give up our lives for him (literally or metaphorically), then we must be willing, whether or not others are walking an apparently easier path.

10. APPLY: In what particular areas are you called to "feed" and "take care of" the sheep? Whether or not we are pastors, most of us have opportunity to feed the sheep in some way—whether that is our children, a Sunday-school class, or the ministry of encouraging one another as brothers and sisters in Christ as we chat over coffee after church. Jesus' emphasis on "feeding" the sheep shows the primary importance of seeking to speak God's word to one another.

• **What difference will it make if you remember that other Christians are Jesus' sheep, not yours?** It is *never* our church; it is Christ's church. We are taking care of his sheep (for him and under his command and tutelage). See 1 Peter 5:1-4. This ought to move us toward great care and gentleness—since people are precious to Jesus, they must be precious to us!

11. APPLY: How can your church move toward being an army that restores its wounded, rather than shooting them? What would need to change? This is an opportunity to come back to some of the issues you discussed in relation to question 1, and apply what you've seen in this passage to the issues raised. Try to really drill down into specifics.

• **How might that play out in your personal relationships with one another?** We will need to be willing to "carry each other's burdens" (Galatians 6:2), to forgive one another, and to welcome the repentant back into our hearts and lives.

12. Think back over everything you've read in John's Gospel. What particular passages have encouraged you personally by showing you...
• **the truth of the gospel (v 24)?**
• **the limitless character of Jesus (v 25)?**
This question is included as a way to review the series (including, if applicable, your studies in John 1 – 12). Allow your group to share what has particularly struck or stuck with them.

Dig deeper into
John's Gospel

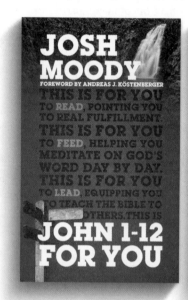
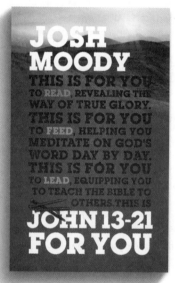

Join Josh Moody as he opens up the Gospel of John, helping you to get to grips with its meaning and showing how it transforms our hearts and lives today. Written for people of every age and stage, from new believers to pastors and teachers, this flexible resource is for you to:

- **Read**: As a guide to the riches of this Gospel, helping you to find and enjoy life to the full.
- **Feed**: As a daily devotional to help you grow in Christ as you read and meditate on this portion of God's word.
- **Lead**: As notes to aid you in explaining, illustrating, and applying John as you preach or lead a Bible study.

Good Book Guides
The full range

BIBLICAL | RELEVANT | ACCESSIBLE

At The Good Book Company, we are dedicated to helping Christians and local churches grow. We believe that God's growth process always starts with hearing clearly what he has said to us through his timeless word—the Bible.

Ever since we opened our doors in 1991, we have been striving to produce Bible-based resources that bring glory to God. We have grown to become an international provider of user-friendly resources to the Christian community, with believers of all backgrounds and denominations using our books, Bible studies, devotionals, evangelistic resources, and DVD-based courses.

We want to equip ordinary Christians to live for Christ day by day, and churches to grow in their knowledge of God, their love for one another, and the effectiveness of their outreach.

Call us for a discussion of your needs or visit one of our local websites for more information on the resources and services we provide.

Your friends at The Good Book Company

thegoodbook.com | thegoodbook.co.uk
thegoodbook.com.au | thegoodbook.co.nz
thegoodbook.co.in